D1590513

# I HATE YOU!

## AN ANGRY MAN'S GUIDE TO REVENGE

M. NELSON CHUNDER

PALADIN PRESS
BOULDER, COLORADO

*I Hate You! An Angry Man's Guide to Revenge*
by M. Nelson Chunder


ISBN 0-87364-278-3
Printed in the United States of America



Published by Paladin Press, a division of
Paladin Enterprises, Inc., P.O. Box 1307,
Boulder, Colorado 80306. (303) 443-7250.

Copies of this book may be purchased from the publisher
for $12.95. All inquiries and catalog requests should
be addressed to Paladin Press. Price may vary following
year of copyright.

Other revenge books from Paladin Press:

*Get Even: The Complete Book of Dirty Tricks*
*Get Even 2: More Dirty Tricks from the Master of Revenge*
*Up Yours! Guide to Advanced Revenge Techniques*
*The Revenge Book*

"Make fun where there is none."

—Gretchen Liscinsky
Sorry Charlie's
Greensburg, PA

# Contents

# Read This First

A few months ago, my friend George Hayduke asked me to take over his literary obligations with Paladin Press relative to this book about getting even with people and institutions who have done you dirty. George told me he was going to Mexico to hunt for Jimmy Hoffa and the men who murdered John Kennedy. He asked me to write this next book for him.

No sweat.

I've been a dirty trickster for about as long as George and I have ridden together.

So, I hope you enjoy what's here. Some of these ideas came from George's files and notes; others are from my sick mind. If you get any new ideas or have some wild stuff you want to share, please send it along to me. I am planning another book, and you could be in it.

Think about it.

Send your ideas anyway.

Cheers,

M. Nelson Chunder
Akron, Ohio

# Additives

There is some magic in the air. Or, as one of my old college friends, a fairly wild hangover from the 1960s, used to say as he dug into his stash . . . "Ahh, better living through chemistry." But, speaking of something completely different, that reminded me of a conversation my brother had with a certain M.M. in Florida.

It seems M.M. is in analysis—as in urine. He notes that if you add methylene blue to various drinks, it will pass through the human body without changing color. I had heard of bluebloods before, but never the other.

# Airlines

Meanwhile, Sorethroat in Orlando, Florida, strings this bit of business together: He got on an airplane and sat quietly with a string hanging out of his mouth. At the end of the string was a small brass ring. Naturally, one of the people seated near him noticed it, but said nothing. A flight attendant finally asked him about the string/ring.

Sorethroat responded in the cultured tone of a studious academic, "I am a research scientist studying the effects of digestive juices on various foods. I recently swallowed a small basket containing samples of raw food. It's on the other end of this string, and I'm about to pull it up now for observation."

That statement cleared the aisles.

This stunt would also work on a bus or train as well.

# Alarm Clocks

If you have access to your mark's bedroom, reset the alarm clock for a time he or she will be asleep. Or, if the mark must get up for work or school, reset the alarm for a later hour. Few people check the time settings, especially if it's a routine schedule situation. This timely tip came from Ron Canaveral in Florida.

# Alarms

Apparently some of the Down Under folks lack a sense of security, as Peter Wanker writes from Sydney that his favorite Australian marks are installing alarms in their homes and autos. He notes, though, that a can of polyurethane foam will silence an alarm horn or bell quickly and quietly for whatever purpose you might have in mind.

On the same subject, that TAP columnist (see Sources), writing as The Stainless Steel Rat, notes that a lot of corporate travelers now carry those personal alarm devices that hang around a metal doorknob. If someone jiggles the knob, the alarm goes off.

"If you find one, hook a piece of wire or other metal object to the outside knob," the Rat writes.

This will cause the alarm to function. Hopefully, the mark will call the hotel desk and security people, which will create a big scene.

Here's a little extra. Before you cause the mark's alarm to go off, tie his/her door to the one across the hall so tightly that he/she cannot open it. Or, tie it to an electrical conduit, water pipe, fire hose or fire alarm.

# Alum

Alum is the natural ingredient in unripe persimmons that causes your mouth to pucker. Powdered alum is readily available on drugstore shelves, too. Replace the mark's salt, sugar, or other seasoning with alum, and watch the fun. This is a good one to use on health-food freaks and in eating establishments. Thank the Indiana Cave Man for this tight-lipped wonderfulness.

# Answering Machines

"Hello, I don't want to talk to you now."

"I'm not at home. Talk to my machine, instead."

The answering machine affair goes on—people and telephones, people vs. machines. For example, every kid on the East Coast at some odd time in his or her career works at "The Shore" during the summer. I did, and it was depressing . . . sex, drugs, and alcohol. That is enough to depress "Pub" who is a real resident of the seaside resort of Wildwood, New Jersey. So, he writes of neat ideas if you hate your mark's answering machine. Or, perhaps, your mark is the machine!

Find out what type/make/model of machine you need to respond to. Beg, borrow, or lift one of the little beepers that activates the answering machine in question. They are all rather interchangeable, according to Pub.

When you know your mark is going to be away and that his or her answering machine will be on, call, and then use your borrowed beeper to erase all his incoming calls. Or, erase only a selected few after you've previewed them. Or, listen to the messages and then revise them. Make up new return messages, or have a friend help you deliver them.

Squatso has another suggestion, if you can get access to the mark's machine. He says, "Get in there and change the outgoing message. Make it awful, direct, gross, insulting." If you want specific suggestions, please write, as Squatso sent me a list of possible messages that propriety prevents me from reproducing here.

# Automobiles

In *Up Yours!*, the author wrote about the Good Samaritan who breaks off toothpicks in car door locks. A fan named Steve offers a refinement of this. He says, "I put a bit of Loctite on both sides of the toothpick before inserting it. I don't push it in the whole way before breaking it off, but I snap it a bit short. Then I use the stub to push it in past the keyhole . . . kind of like countersinking."

A reader signing himself "The Big Con," writes from Cignetti, West Virginia, that he likes to do this same thing, only he applies this technique to the ignition lock.

"That's a real nasty one, something I would do only to someone who really deserved it," Big Con writes.

To pull off this next one, says Doug German, your mark either has to have two cars parked in tandem or have his/her car in a parking lot. Take fifty-pound test or stronger fishing line, wrap one end around the back bumper of the car, and wrap the other to the front gate of the vehicle in front. Wrap several layers of line. Doug reports one mark spent sixty dollars to replace his car's front grate after this stunt.

A simple variation on this same idea would be to attach a two-by-four stud, fulcrum-type arrangement, under the fender, slanted toward the rear of the vehicle. We can thank Bob Marchhairsani, a former university poster child from Philadelphia, Pennsylvania, for that idea.

Morton Downey, Jr., wasn't shy as he told me, "Don't even ask me why I did this to the guy, he was such a jerk. Trust me, this mark deserved it!"

Here's what happened. The mark had bought a new car and was a gas mileage nut. So, each night, Morton would add a few gallons of gasoline to the mark's car, unknown, of course, to the sucker. The mark took the car into the garage for the usual new-car checkup at five hundred miles. He bragged about his fabulous 70-MPG record. The service people looked at him oddly, as this car was rated by the EPA at 35 MPG.

"Then, I dropped the other pedal," Morton related. "I snuck around each night and siphoned out a few gallons, taking a little more each time. He had to get his tank filled more and more often."

By now, irate at the drop in gas efficiency, the mark took his car to the garage six times, screaming how his mileage had dropped through the 40s to the 20s and was now about 15 MPG.

Kilroy is a lot less kind. He starts his stunt with the hood of the mark's car already raised in symbolic surrender. While under the hood of your mark's car, locate the coil and attach a length of greasy bell wire to the negative terminal. Use old, greasy wire so it won't look out of place. Attach the other end of the wire to a ground. Your mark will not be able to start the car, and I don't know of any mechanic who can figure this one out!

Here's another of Kilroy's brilliant ideas. While driving through a parking lot, did you ever encounter someone blocking traffic as he or she waits for a car to pull out close to the store so as to avoid walking those few extra yards? Here's how to deal with them. Go to your local wrecking yard and find a car with an intact windshield-washer system. Purchase it, and install that extra system in your car. Take the washer nozzles that ejaculate water on the windshield and attach them to your car's grille—pointing straight forward. You may need some extra tubing to complete this task. It is available from your local aquarium store. Once the system is installed, fill the reservoir with thinned paint. The next time someone blocks you in the parking lot, you can flip on the switch and give them Kilroy's designer paint job on the rear end of their car.

# Banks

No lover of the honest life, and an ex-biker, Joey Kiechci says that you can get your mark in trouble by soaking a bank with secondary markdom.

"The deal is to write a note on the back of a deposit slip you know your mark will use. That's not all that tough to do if you think about it. Anyway, the note says, *'This is a stickup. I got a gun in my pocket and I'll blow your brains all over the wall unless you give me all the money,'* or something equally awful. As he innocently hands the marked deposit slip to the teller, he will not hear the silent bells, but he'll see stripes in his new wardrobe."

You and I know he won't really be arrested and will never see prison. But there will be a lot of hassle, threat, loud talk, and enough nastiness to share between the mark and his bank. Or, ex-bank, perhaps.

# Barking Dogs

What's that, you say your neighbor's dogs bark? Your grandpa's old remedy used to be to shoot the dog with a BB gun. Here's a better idea. Call the neighbor and tell him/her you just spotted some kids lurking outside. Of course, you have to be sure the dog is just a barker, a mutt who likes to hear its own voice. Now, when the uncaring neighbor goes outside to check, you must lurk nearby with a lightly charged airgun and—you guessed it—nail the cacophonous canine's owner right square on her or his butt.

# Blood (Fake)

My thanks to Dr. Foge McCutcheon for this sensational substitute with so many uses. Combine ferric chloride and potassium thiocyanate solutions to produce a bright red liquid that looks just like blood.

# Blood (Real)

Wait, don't be squeamish. Good grief, I was twenty-two years old before I knew there were other uses for a hemostat. Read what the Indiana Cave Man has to say about this topic, as I think you'll like the vein his humor runs in.

Get some real animal blood from a slaughterhouse. Freeze a large chunk of it, and keep it packed in dry ice until you're ready to stash it in the mark's desk drawer, filing cabinet, briefcase, locker, safe deposit box, mailbox, etc. It's especially effective if the enclosure is lockable and the mark is absent. When a pool of blood is discovered dripping from a locked container, someone is *sure* to call the police, who will harass the mark for several hours, after which he has a nasty mess to clean up. The boss's rug is an ideal place for a mishap to occur. If you can't transfer a brick of frozen blood into the mark's possession, use a large syringe, enema set, etc., to inject the liquid.

# Bolts

Want to help your mark by stripping some of the vital bolts on his equipment, home or other property? Kilroy suggests you use a sixteen-point box end wrench two sizes larger than the bolt; torque it down very tight.

# Bombs

Even unreal bombs are fun, especially if you are a master of disguise. You can buy empty cases for practice bombs at most military surplus stores and fill them with materials that look like explosives. Many high explosives look like brown wax or plastic wood fillers. Other experts have said that brown sugar looks like an explosive, too.

Buy an empty practice bomb case and fill it with bogus explosive. You'll have to paint the outer case for realism, too. Most practice units are blue, so you need to paint yours flat black, with an inch-and-a-half yellow band about six inches from the end.

Partly bury it nose-down in the ground of your mark's lawn, or lean it against the door of his or her office. You can also hide it so that it will surely be found—in the broom closet or basement of the home or office.

Caution: Leave no fingerprints or other trackable clues, as police and military bomb-disposal people have little sense of humor about this sort of trick. A very understandable emotion, I'd agree.

# Born Agains

The Rev. Martin Newcumer Holmes, a lay minister in the order of St. Mattress, has published a list of different ways to harass Born Agains who are bothering you. His list appeared in *Overthrow* magazine, an excellent publication. The list:

1. Shout "Bring back the Roman lions" at them.
2. Have a mass Bible-burning at one of their street meetings.
3. Request that the church grant space for a mass divine bisexual penetration, i.e., orgy.
4. Make a citizen's arrest of any Born-Again preacher you find, charging him with promoting obscenity.
5. Tell them loudly that you're a born-again pervert.
6. Tell them you're a gay activist and you would like to teach Sunday School to lead their kids in the right direction.
7. Spray-paint a lavender hammer and sickle on the church doors.
8. Telephone the preacher at 4 A.M., stating the Communists are "out to get" you.
9. Have a mass nude baptism in the name of born-again perversion.

10. Disrupt a church service by exclaiming that the Bible is a bunch of racist and sexist fairy tales.
11. Ask them if God has a penis or a vagina.
12. Pass out tracts stating that Jesus can be seen via the use of LSD, peyote, or mushrooms.
13. Tell them you have X-ray vision which allows you to see through their clothes.
14. Squirt them with a solution of DMSO and LSD.
15. Stamp their right hand or forehead with the numbers, "666."
16. Start your own O.R.G.A.S.M. chapter (Organization of Religious Groups Against Sexual Materials). Pass out explicitly written antiporn literature written in the style of a sleazy skin book.
17. Call in on any religious audience participation programs on radio or TV and give every detail of your depraved life before being Born Again.
18. Organize a Jump for Jesus rally with the local parachute club.

# Bumper Stickers

I hope you won't be "offendered," but I found a source that prints bumper stickers for you. As they note in their ad copy, "Yes, you send us the wording you want, and we'll print it." That's fair enough. The rest of their ad promises long-life, self-stick vinyl. See "Walter Drake & Sons" in the Source section.

# Buried Treasure

Jim Murray of Columbia, South Carolina, relayed a funny idea on a WIS radio talk show. Bury a few trinkets of lookalike gold on the mark's property, and then create the publicity that *real* valuable stuff has been found there. If the mark has a farm or large, open land, so much the better. However, I can see this one also being used for a city tenement building. Think about this a little bit.

You can also use buried treasure to terrorize other people. If you're in a treasure-hunting area, such as a beach or fairgrounds in which people armed with metal detectors prowl after busy weekends, add some excitement to their lives.

Bury a small unlocked box in a shallow hole and tamp it down well. You might even tamp some sod on it if necessary. The treasure hunter finds the treasure and eagerly digs it up. The payoff is now up to you. Here are some suggestions from Lucy Chamber, the lady who suggested all this nastiness in the first place:

1. The small box is festooned with official-looking United States Government Radiation Warning stickers.
2. The small box contains an especially disgusting piece of roadkill.

3. If you can specify which individual mark will open the small box, you could stuff a recently dead house pet belonging to that mark into the box.
4. If the treasure hunters are little kids, you could fill the small box with porno pictures the rug rats can take back to mommy.

# Calcium Carbide

We had an old uncle back East who used to be a deep miner in West Virginia. In the old days, mines were lighted by carbide lamps, and many hardware stores in mine country across this nation still sell carbide, along with helmets that have carbide lamps built right into the hat. It is also used by nocturnal hunters and campers.

Calcium carbide is available where camping supplies are sold. It looks like crushed rock. It produces large volumes of acetylene gas when it comes into contact with water. The acetylene contains hydrogen sulfide and other impurities, and it has a nauseating smell. Here are some uses:

1. Distribute carbide in the mark's locale. It reacts slowly with atmospheric moisture and produces a long-lasting, low-level stench.
2. Add carbide to the mark's potted plants. It will really take off next time the plants are watered, and it will probably kill the plants as well.
3. Carefully dry the bowl of a water fountain or sink, or the floor of a shower stall; add carbide. Watch the fun when the mark turns on the water. Caution: acetylene gas is explosive in a wide range of mixtures in the air. A plastic trash bag filled

with acetylene and oxygen from a welding set sounds like a stick of dynamite when ignited. Use a long fuse.

# Candy

Here's another horrible idea from our Aussie friend, Tug Wanker. He says to add some internal twists to the *Up Yours!* suggestion of turning human fecal matter into candy, using dog droppings instead.

"If you have a mark who has abused an animal, this is very fitting revenge. You help the animal because it can't help itself," Wanker says.

"Get some dog crap and let it dry. Put on rubber gloves and cut the stuff into small squares. Melt some milk chocolate and pour it over the feces. Once dry, wrap the pieces in foil and place in an empty candy box. In addition to the immediate effect, the 'candy' is likely to give the mark a case of internal parasites. Ask any veterinarian about this."

I did ask, and I got some of the strangest looks you can imagine, along with "You can't be serious. Do you realize how sick that could make someone?"

It all sounds like good news to me.

# Car Dealers

Mot Rot has an excellent idea to help prospective buyers decide whether to buy from your mark—the salesperson.

"A water pistol full of motor oil and black coloring that's squirted through the front grille of a showroom vehicle in question gives the buyer a lot to think about when he peeks under the hood," Mot reports.

# Car Pounds

I bet nearly all of you have had or will have your car towed away. It isn't one of life's fun experiences. It's where you learn fast about the tough, real world of uncaring greed. But, there's a brighter outlook, thanks to Kilroy.

"Want to get even with the car pound? Want to get a free paint job?" he asks.

Here's his scam. Park your car in a towaway zone. It is soon towed. It's vital that your car was never towed there before or the authorities will grow suspicious at what's about to happen.

Late that night, using one of those old-fashioned, pump-type fire extinguishers or a garden sprayer filled with paint, shower all the cars in the pound with odd and grossly colored paint. You can travel the outside perimeter of the fence, spraying the paint up, over, and around.

If the yard has a guard dog, feed it drugged meat, then spray it, too. Even if they put up a legal bluff, the yard is really responsible for your car and all of the others while they are impounded. That is why these yards are bonded. They will have no choice but to fix your car to your liking.

"I have personally done this one," Kilroy notes. "It is one of the most profitable and rewarding acts of vengeful vandalism I have ever experienced. I've always gotten what I asked for."

# CB Wars

Moronic barbarians that they are, CBers tend to fight among themselves. There are many documented cases of heavy violence resulting from arguments over stepping on messages, use of a particular channel, or because a CBer caught up with someone who had bad-mouthed him on the air or jammed his transmissions. If you know the internal details of a CB war and have a CB of your own, there are things you can do to escalate the conflict:

1. Jam selectively so that the jamee blames some other mark.
2. Tape-record and rebroadcast "select" transmissions or create new ones.
3. Build a short-range jammer from a cheap toy CB walkie-talkie. Hide it near the mark's house, where it will jam "his" channel. Use a large battery so it will run for a long time. Remove all fingerprints. Enclose a nasty note to the mark, in case he finds the jammer. Sign some other mark's name.

Although I would hardly class it in the same sexually symbolic terms that many readers do, the CBer's antenna is surely his most vulnerable point for physical attack. I would like to add a suggestion from the Indiana Cave Man, who notes, "Always be sure to tie your tow or other dragging-away device to the feed line so that the mark's radio is dragged through the nearest window, smashed up against the wall, or torn right out of the car when the main antenna goes on its sudden departure."

You can also cut the feed line in two places so that it is too short to splice. That way the mark has to buy an entire new length and hook it up.

Or, as the ex-CBer Wild Willy noted, "Many mobile antennas unscrew at the base, which is attached to the vehicle. Just loosen the antenna a lot so that it will fall off as the mark drives away."

# Cement

If you have, can get, or can buy access to a load of wet, ready-mix cement bound for the mark's construction site, you can add fluorescein, roadkill, feces, or butyric acid, as appropriate. Better yet, add some large bones, human if possible, to the concrete, and be sure no-nonsense authorities are notified just after the load arrives and is poured.

# Charcoal Grill

The Tennessean has a bang-up idea for your mark's next cookout party. He says to take an ordinary twelve-gauge shotgun shell and cut it apart at the wadding. This way you'll get rid of all the BBs. Use good-quality electrical tape to wrap around and around the shell husk. Mix Elmer's glue with charcoal dust and keep recoating the taped-over shell until you get something that looks amazingly like a charcoal briquet. Put it back in your mark's charcoal bucket or bag. You could also put several of these little time bombs in there. There's nothing like starting that next cookout with a *bang*, eh?

# Charity

I thought it would be nice to add something positive in this case. Could we volunteer the mark for all sorts of religious and other charity work? Let's pretend to be his or her secretary calling to volunteer the *biggie* for some community service. Or, using official letterhead, let's do the same thing. Try to make the service as common, little guy and/or demeaning as possible. Try to tie up his or her weekends. Usually, the majority of "marked" upperfolks will just do their day in the barrel rather than raise too much fuss. On the other hand, if they bitch too much, it hurts their reputation even more. Heads you lose, tails I win.

# Chickens

After reading Ted Shumaker's contribution, I'm not sure I will ever order Chicken a la King again. A fisherman, Ted takes along a glass jar that's full of chicken intestines to use as bait. He once tightly sealed an extra jar, stuck it in his car trunk and forgot about it. The chicken intestines fermented and exploded, sending a mixture of chicken guts-'n-glass shrapnel all through his trunk.

"I had that car three years and never did get the awful smell out of the trunk," Ted says. "No spray invented, no cleaner—commercial or otherwise—worked. No freshener hid the odor. It was awful."

As a youngster I cleaned my share of chickens and I can vouch for what they smell like fresh. I can only imagine the fowl odor described by Ted. Perhaps, Chicken Tartare would be on order? Forget it, it was a joke.

# Churches

Not too long ago, I did a radio talk show in Orlando, Florida. A lady who said she wanted to be known as Fragrance called in to talk about the Catholic Church. She was an older lady, the type you always thought of as straight and no-nonsense. Delightfully, I was very wrong. She was wonderful.

"A long, long time ago, my sister and I put a strong ink in the Holy Water, and because the church was very dark then with little lighting, a lot of people ended up with the ink-spot look."

There was no suggestion for this, it's just neat that a truly senior citizen has the same sense of humor to share all these years later.

# Cigarettes

Jim Fisher runs a very cool radio talk show out of WOC in Davenport, Iowa. That reminds me of a great idea from Donald Murphy of that city.

"This guy bums smokes all the time . . . disgusting, cheap jerk. I took some filtered Kools and buried a matchhead in the middle of a Kool for the next time he bummed one from me.

"That mixture of sulphur and menthol didn't really flame, but it ruined his taste buds for a couple days," says Donald.

# Classified Advertising

I read my newspapers most thoroughly and found these two classified ads running a few times. I wonder if they are straight? If not, I am sure each crafty reader can immediately create a great scam from each.

1. Tired of finding time to do your grocery shopping? Let me do it for you. I will shop, find all the bargains, then deliver to you. Phone __________.
2. I would like to talk seriously with anyone who was foolish enough to buy contact lenses from __________. If you were taken, too, call __________.

If you're feeling smug by now, let me introduce Panama's own R. P. Ork, who knows which classified buttons to push, sending his mark down the slide to confusion and unhappiness. Ork says, "I find that for guys, the two greatest things to advertise are guns and cars, especially if you sell mint classics of each at a fair, or less, price.

"Everyone reading the ad is looking for a bargain or better. So, give better to him. And, stick it to your mark, too. It's easy," says Ork.

Here's Ork's order of battle for this one. Select a weekend you know your mark will be at home and, hopefully, be entertaining guests or be otherwise busy. Then, place your ad in a newspaper or have it read on the radio for him.

"Let's advertise an S & W .44 mag, with 8¾ inch barrel, new-in-box, for just $300. Say it's a sacrifice to make a mortgage payment," advises Ork.

"Or, advertise a collector's model Ford T-Bird, 1957, better-than-mint, for only $7,000 because of a divorce settlement due now."

According to Ork, the stinger here is that you advertise on the weekend when the mark can't readily stop the ad; you don't include a telephone number, just an address, and you ask people to come at an hour you know will be upsetting to your mark. Also, your mark will have to argue with the newspaper or radio station about not paying for the advertising for which he's being billed.

# Communist Propaganda

Listen to Radio Moscow/Havana/Peking on a shortwave radio. Write down their mailing addresses and send them letters of great praise from the mark requesting QSL cards, program schedules, and other literature. They read these types of letters from listeners over the air, so send "good ones" from the mark, making him sound like an active supporter.

The mark will receive a big load of propaganda and will also get his name recorded in the computers of the CIA, FBI and other interested institutions filed under possible Commies, subversives, and other bad stuff. This is useful against politicians, those in the military, bigots, Moral-Majority types, and marks who have security clearances.

# Computers

Jimmy Carter, no, not that one, is a fine duster, suggesting if you have a grudge against a computer-using operator that you sprinkle a bit of fine sand on the hard discs they use for data storage and retrieval. At best, the disc will shatter, and at high speeds, those little pieces will scatter all through the unit.

Are you savoring the down time already?

# Condoms

I was going to slip this on as a stunt under the automobile section, but I figured condom would attract more attention. Now that I have yours—attention, that is—here's the deal. This one came in from The Tennessean out there in Savannah. Unroll a fresh condom and place it inside the gas tank of the mark's car, pushing it down in with a wire. The Tennessean says the rubber will float around in there until it gets sucked up into the gas line, in which case it won't get too far, causing the engine to die. Sometimes, the condom floats free and the car starts again and runs. Sometimes, it doesn't. Either way, it's fun for you; hell for the mark.

When it comes to releasing a flood of feeling about friends and marks, Florida's E. G. doesn't fool around. He fills a strong, brand-name quality condom with a gallon or so of iced water and then gently lays it down next to his mark who may be sleeping or in a drunken stupor. The next loud step is to have the alarm go off or the telephone ring on that appropriate (other) side of the mark.

# Crickets

Crickets are great assets. Infesting your mark's habitat with myriads of crickets can be an investment with unusually high yield. These little guys can be caught in the field near your place and kept in small cages, or you can buy them at most bait shops. Not only do they chirp loudly and hop around, they eat holes in many fabrics. Also, a cricket can look like a cockroach to many people. It seems to me that crickets would be good to use against die-hard environmentalists who refuse to use insecticides.

# Dates

I can't understand why someone would want to get rid of a date or gross out someone else's date that very night. But if you do, Morton Downey, Jr., has a workable plan acquired from his own experience during a double-date dinner in a fine restaurant.

"It was a situation that called for a quick gross-out and riddance, believe me," says Morton. "While the other folks' attention was diverted, I stuffed a bunch of fried onions up my nose and into my mouth. I then faked a huge, loud, animated sneeze, spraying the target-date with mist, slime, and solids. The after-action report was that I still had a variety of the onions hanging out of my nostrils and mouth. The stunt was totally effective; she split."

# Desk Drawers

Thanks to WOC radio's Jim Fisher in Davenport, Iowa, I learned of one manager who was frustrated with his terminally dumb office help and their attempts to ruin his career and decided to play musical drawers with his staff.

"I arrived very early one morning and switched their desk drawers around from desk to desk. Then I left and called in at 8 A.M. that I'd be in a bit late. I had a great breakfast and then walked in to find all the stupid jerks in a mess over whose drawer belonged in whose desk. They were still trying to figure it out thirty minutes later," says the manager.

"I often thought how much fun it would have been to add a bit of super glue to the trick!"

# Dog Droppings

If you have a dog owner who allows his pet to poop on your premises, a WOC radio listener in Davenport has a grand idea—give the gift back.

"Borrow some paper from a local store or use your imagination. Wrap the fresh crap in lots of paper stuffing, put it in a decorator box, and gift-wrap it," advises the listener. "Put on a nice bow and card. Then have the package delivered, or mail it to your mark. Hopefully, the mark will fish around in the packing for the present."

Is that what the Pointer Sisters meant by a soft touch?

# Doorknobs

Doorknobs and small alcohol burners make interesting companions. You can obtain a small burner for a very nominal sum in any hobby store. Construct a wire frame for the burner and hang it on the outside of your mark's doorknob so that the flame from the burner makes strong, direct contact with the knob.

The idea here is to do this for fifteen or twenty minutes before the mark will open the door, either on some schedule, such as jogging or work, or because you have pushed a doorbell button. Within those fifteen or twenty minutes of cooking, the heat will radiate to the inside knob, which your mark will soon grasp. It's not a really nice way to start his or her day!

If this idea warms you up, you'll have to hand the credit to Kilroy.

# Drinking Fountains

A generic thought about plumbing fixtures could concern drinking fountains and goes like this.

"No children, dwarfs, or other handicapped folks work in my office. Yet, the other fountain is about eighteen inches off the floor, making it tough to drink from," writes our composite complainer.

"So, I bought a very official-looking custom sign (from a mail-order house in another state) and placed it above the fountain. It read:

UNISEX URINAL/BIDET
DRINK AT YOUR OWN RISK

Also, according to Norton Worthen, an unemployed commode designer, you can use a small hex wrench to turn a fountain's nozzle so it will spray the user in the face—hard.

"You can also adjust the flow so that the person has to suck on the device itself, which means you could treat that part of the unit with chemicals and other awful things," Worthen relates.

Other suggestions came from The Indiana Cave Man, who suggested wrapping fluorescein, potassium permanganate, or another potent dye in a nylon stocking and cramming it into the nozzle area on down the pipe behind the nozzle.

Finally, Ruthless Love, a member of the Pagans, a great bunch of bikers, suggested putting something terminally disgusting into the fountain's bowl, e.g., old vegetable soup tinged with butyric acid, a week's collection of nose blow, some dead rodents, the severed head of a house cat, a dead bird, an obviously used condom, a dirty woman's used panties, etc.

# Eating Out the Slobs

A wonderful waitress from Davenport told me a great way to correct pigs who hassle the ladies who wait on them in restaurants:

"If the guy is a real jerk and just won't let you alone, then it's time to get someone else to distract him awhile. Usually, you have one waitress who has a great, healthy chest, or one who knows crude jokes, or one with Jane Fonda Class Legs. While the jerk has his mind caught in his pants zipper, you run out to his car and run a line of dirty grease on his steering wheel and heavy syrup on the car seat. He is a sloppy slob in your place, so let's pay him back accordingly. The punishment fits the crime."

# Electrical Appliances

Kilroy has a home decorator's suggestion on how to help your mark exercise the circuit breakers and his or her own health, and also make an appliance repairperson richer.

"Cut the plug off a favored appliance—after you detach it from the wall receptacle. Tie the two wires together and tape with electrical tape to prevent a visible flash. Plug the armed cord into the outlet behind a piece of heavy furniture and wait for him/her to turn the appliance on. After your mark resets his blown circuit breakers umpteen times, a frustrated phone call will ring out for the expensive repairperson."

More from Kilroy: This time, unplug the mark's TV, stereo, vacuum cleaner, etc. Push a straight pin through the cord to create a short circuit. Use wire cutters to cut off the protruding ends of the pin so that the mark can't see the pin. When the mark sticks the plug in an outlet, there will be a big flash and puff of smoke. The fuse blows or the circuit breaker opens, leaving the outlet dead.

If the mark is a true nerd, he will refuse to believe that something is wrong with his precious equipment and will probably try plugging it into another outlet or two before giving up and going to a repair shop. Line cords rarely go bad, so the repair shop will probably replace many of the appliance's expensive guts before testing the cord. It's standard practice in even the best repair shops to charge the mark for everything that was replaced while attempting to find the trouble.

In the meantime, the poor mark (now there is a contradiction of terms), will be screaming, "Watt's wrong with my electrical circuits? Has the devil possessed me and my home?"

The Indiana Cave Man has invented a splendid tool for electrical chicanery. He calls it his Handy Dandy Fuse Popper (HDFP). It's an ordinary male plug with its terminals shorted together with very heavy wire, probably ten or twelve gauge. You simply shove this plug into selected outlets in the mark's home or office, and then remove it promptly after it does its ominous task, which leaves the mark with a dead outlet. This is fun, as it does nice things to the minds of paranoid marks.

An electric company's watt-hour meters are sealed against tampering by a special plastic or metal padlock-shaped device which is easily removed with a pair of wire cutters. Removing the seal is illegal. If you remove the seal from the mark's meter, he'll never notice, but the meter reader will. The power company will probably replace the seal once or twice and say nothing, but if the seal repeatedly disappears, the mark will get in trouble about it.

If you want to be less subtle, you can simply rip off the seal and metal retaining band, unplug the entire meter assembly, and smash it to the ground, simultaneously depriving the mark of power and getting him and the power company angry with each other. The company may even hold him responsible for the costly device.

You could also remove the seal and meter while the mark is away, tamper crudely with the insides, and replace the meter. The mark won't notice, but the power company will, and they'll come down hard on him.

Here's another idea: Remove the mark's meter and exchange it with some other mark's meter. Choose meters with vastly different readings. Both marks will get whopping bills—the mark whose meter reading was less than last time will get charged for 100,000+ kilowatt-hours, because the power company's computer will assume that the meter made a full revolution. If you leave the swap as is, the power company will accuse the marks of hanky-panky. If you undo the swap after the meter reader has made his rounds, the billing fiasco will be repeated next month, and the only evidence will be a couple of missing seals. Trying to convince the power company that *they* made a mistake will keep the two marks busy for weeks!

If the mark's electric service is in an isolated area, shoot the meter with a bow and arrow, crossbow, or shotgun when there are no witnesses around. You could also stick a Nazi pike or some other symbolic spear into it. When the meter is replaced, attack it again. After losing a few meters, the power company can legally refuse to supply service to the mark.

# Electronic Equipment

Piezoelectric spark-shooters are made for lighting gas flames. They're inexpensive and available where camping equipment is sold. When the trigger is pulled, many thousands of volts are generated which jump a half-inch gap at the end. The volts could shock you, but only very mildly. Modify one of these sparkers by extending the tip and surrounding shell with a pair of wires, needles, etc. Insert the end into the mark's electronic equipment and start shooting sparks into the integrated circuits. This causes untraceable device failure and is especially effective against computers, especially while they are operating. If this idea shocks you, thank the Indiana Cave Man.

# Enemies

One of the finest pieces of advice I got came from this wonderful lady in central Florida who told me, "Always forgive your enemies; nothing bothers them so much."

# Farm Animals

Everyone loves to see farm animals. In the spring, entire families spend weekends gazing at tiny sheep and cattle. If your mark owns a herd of cattle or sheep, you can surely give the fans a message. Using epoxy spray paint, which won't harm the critters, spray obscene messages and sexual commands on the sides of the animals. This paint is very hard to remove from their fur and is very readable, especially if you use the Day-Glow varieties.

You could probably accuse your mark of some form of participatory bestiality, such as identifying small sheep as his offspring or using spray paint on the side of a cow to say that your mark was the worst lay she'd ever had. Stuff like that can be funny, especially when the little rug rats start asking mommy and daddy what all the words written on the animals mean.

# Fast Food Places

This one is sure to generate a bad taste somewhere. Pick a food chain in your area with lots of outlets. For example, drive up to one branch of your local McFastfood. Order something. Pay the two dollars, or whatever, and drive to their next outlet. Order something different and much more expensive.

When the young lady gives you your bill, pay and leave. Drive back in thirty seconds and present the first bag of goodies and your larger check. Ask for a mammoth refund. Then enjoy your discount meal.

# Fireplaces

This one also works well with wood stoves and comes to us with the goodwill of the Tennessean. Actually, it's also an old World War II trick from the British Special Operations Executive. Maybe the Tennessean is an old SOE man?

Take a piece of firewood from your mark's woodpile or get one log like the type he uses. In your home or shop, drill a one-inch hole about twelve inches deep. Insert an M-80, some other large firecracker, or a cut-down skyrocket into that hole. Repack with shavings and sawdust after using Elmer's glue to fasten the explosive device in the cavity. Close the end with glue and/ or putty. Smear some light clay on that end of the log and allow it to harden. Replace the special "log" on top of the mark's woodpile. You may never hear about it, but the mark surely will.

# Fluorescein

Remember that orange dye marker my friend George Hayduke and some friends used in a community swimming pool to teach some bigots a lesson? I didn't know this, but the technical name for that substance is fluorescein, and it's available at chemical supply houses. You can also get it by buying surplus dye-marker kits at an Army/Navy store. It's an intense yellow dye which turns bright green in sunlight. It's harmless, but upsetting, especially when it's put into a village or private water supply, ornamental fountain, swimming pool, etc.

Here are some ideas for its use from The Indiana Cave Man. He uses a salt shaker with closable holes. If the mark is a housewife or janitor, sprinkle some fluorescein on the tile or linoleum floor. The more they try to mop it away, the greener it glows.

If you sprinkle it into a carpet, it is almost impossible to get rid of. Normally highly water-soluble, it really stains porous items. The Cave Man also suggests that you add butyric acid to the fluorescein and place the mixture in a newly poured, wet concrete area, such as a porch, patio, or flooring slab.

You can sprinkle it on clothes (for sweat to mix with) or on bathing suits. Sprinkle it on doormats so kids track it inside. Put it in the bottled water at the office.

# Food

Boise Jim had had it. He was tired of the horrible food served in his school cafeteria. "It was so bad," he wrote, "that even Reagan's EPA was concerned about cleaning up the place." Jim didn't wait for the bureaucrats.

"I found my salvation in a coin machine in the rest room of a local bar. I bought some cheap generic condoms. I thought I might add some spice to the clam chowder," Jim says.

Ever the gourmet, I wondered if Jim meant Manhattan or New England. Nevertheless, here's how he slipped the condomint into the chowder.

"It was a buffet line, serve yourself. As I poured clam chowder into my bowl, I simply touched the ladle to the opened rubber, and presto—it stuck. I just put the laden-ladle back in the tureen. About two minutes later, some young cutie poured the rubber into her bowl. Her reaction was certainly funnier than that of the stiff teachers."

The same bit of creative cookery works well in any buffet-style eating place. Remember, where you serve yourself, you may always serve others.

# Garbage

If your city is having a garbage collector's strike, and they're about as common today as business failures, here's a way to use the strike to get one up on your mark. Obtain as much of your mark's trash as possible, making sure you add as many especially gross and disgusting things as you can (like human feces, used sexual accessories, child porno stuff, etc.). Collect this yourself, and set it aside, as Julia Child would say. Let it develop character and odor.

Now write some nasty protest letters to various civic leaders in your mark's name. Get abusive and threatening. Mail the letters. Put carbon copies and other items containing your mark's name and address in your simmering garbage bags. Take these bags to the city park, a freeway overpass, city hall, or the mayor's home. Bomb the stuff there and get away quickly.

Nature, law, and official retaliation will take their course.

# Gas Stations

If you know a true creep who owns a gas station, one in a chain of a major oil company, for example, Mot Rot knows a good pay-back. Mot says that the underground storage tank for unleaded gas at the mark's station is a fine place for you to dump your leaded gas.

Mot reports, "Leaded gas found in an unleaded storage tank is very illegal and conviction carries a heavy fine. Modern tests can easily determine even small amounts of lead." Mot says to put this modern technology to work on your behalf.

# Getaway

One author, Ronald George Eriksen 2, has a book called *Getaway* (available from Paladin Press). Some of his ideas may help remove you and your vehicle from the scene.

1. Have thorough knowledge of the area you are driving in.
2. Predrive all avenues, and note possible escape routes and side exits.
3. Avoid getting boxed-in in traffic.
4. Always park so you have a fast exit from your parking space.
5. If possible, drive on major thoroughfares.
6. Know the locations of police stations, hospitals, military outposts, etc.
7. Check rear-view mirrors frequently.
8. Be wary of groups of men in uniform (jogging suits, janitor outfits, etc.).
9. Look for walkie talkie units.
10. Never trust anyone with your automobile key.
11. Avoid construction areas.
12. Keep your gas tank at least half full.
13. If suspicious people are observed loitering about your vehicle, avoid it.

If you think, though, that you are being followed, using Ronald Eriksen's book, here are some modified suggestions to lose that tail. As some of these are fairly extreme and involve illegal and perhaps unsafe techniques, please be sure you *do* have a tail before you start this drill. There is no sense in attracting undue attention to yourself and your vehicle.

1. After running a red light or driving the wrong way on a one-way street, watch to see if anyone follows.
2. While traveling on a freeway at high speed, suddenly cut across four lanes of traffic and make an exit.
3. After rounding a blind curve, make a bootlegger's turn and take off in the opposite direction.
4. After turning a corner, pull over and park. Take note of all vehicles passing by.
5. Go through alleys, dirt roads, sidewalks, or cut across people's lawns.
6. While driving over a long undivided bridge, suddenly make a bootlegger's turn.
7. Have a *very* trusted friend follow you to detect any surveillance.

# Golf Balls

There was this rumor going around back when we were kids that if you put mothballs in your vehicle's gasoline tank it hopped up the power of the car. I don't know if that's true, but the following idea that came in from several people surely is true.

Put an ordinary golf ball into the gas tank of your mark's car. The ball rolls with the motion of the vehicle, going "bump" each time it hits the edge of the tank in any direction. Your mark will keep wondering, "What in hell is that soft bump, bump, bump I keep hearing?"

Some of the newer cars which use unleaded gas probably don't have a large enough opening to fit a golf ball. How about a ball bearing? Or several ball bearings? They'd make a louder bump anyway.

# Golfers

Kilroy told me about getting even with this gruesome slob who used to bug, bait, and cheat at golf. It's a good story, even though the actual payoff is typical of two-dollar-haircut humor.

"This obese sap used to think he'd lose weight and get strong carrying his light golf bag and a few clubs around when a bunch of us played on Sunday afternoon.

"Trust me, the guy is such a horror show he gives slobs a good name. Anyway, I placed a ten-pound iron weight from an exercise set in the bottom of his bag. By the fifth hole, the guy is muttering and bitching about his bag getting heavier and heavier. That gave me an idea.

"The following week I wrapped another weight in a towel and put it in the bottom of the bag. This guy staggered through the nine holes, sweat popping out of his fat face, giving his porcine pallor an unhealthy pall.

"He didn't show up the next week."

# Graffiti

Here is some arousing new literary mulch for the spray-paint and marker crowd. The following graffiti are new from my own collection and that of other Movement loyalists. Credit is given where appropriate. You'll find no special order to this collection, and you are welcome to borrow and use each as your own. Spray in peace, as they say.

GETTING UP EARLY IN THE MORNING IS WORSE THAN GOING TO BED WITH A MAN WHO DOESN'T KNOW WHAT HE'S DOING

—Diane, in Jessick, IN, 1983

PISS ON DISCO
I SNATCH KISSES AND VICE VERSA
—Woodland Lounge, a biker's bar in PA, 1982

SPERM BANK NIGHT DEPOSIT
SIT ON A HAPPY FACE

—O'Hare, Chicago, 1982

NEVER STEP IN ANYTHING SOFT
THE BIGGER THEY ARE THE HARDER THEY HIT

—Paul Wilson in CO, 1983

CONSERVE PAPER, USE BOTH SIDES
—Jimmy Watt in Washington, 1983

VOTE NO ON PROPOSITION YES
—R. Wilson Reagan in NJ, 1983

WE'RE SNOW BLIND . . . DO ANOTHER LINE
—P. Chico in Salvador, 1983

REALITY IS FOR THOSE WHO CAN'T HANDLE DRUGS
—John Mitchell in Eglin AFB, 1976

I GAVE HER A DIAMOND, SHE GAVE ME A DISEASE
—Tracy in PA, 1982

PABST IS MY BREW HEAVEN
—David in Honduras, 1983

I'M RIPE, EAT ME
—Mick in St. Louis, 1983

BUILDERS HAVE GREAT TOOLS
—Paul Wilson in Boulder, 1981

HUMPTY-DUMPTY WAS ON THE GRASSY KNOLL
—R. Nixxon in Dallas, 1963

HOW DO *YOU* SPELL RELIEF? F-A-R-T!
—Uncle Gerald in Pittsburgh, forever

I'M NOT WEARING UNDERWEAR,
FILM AT 11

—D. Hazinski in Atlanta, 1983

GOOD SEX IS NEVER HAVING TO
SAY YOU'RE HORNY

—Dreamers Everywhere

# Halloweeners

Mike "No More Mr. Nice Guy" McCoochen did the following to pay back some teenage hooligans who enjoyed smashing little kids' pumpkins in the street.

Mike rigged a light socket to a board behind a huge pumpkin. He attached an M-80 to the filament of a 150-watt light bulb. This socket was attached to a switch which disconnected the flow of electricity when pressure was applied.

"When the nasty mark lifts the pumpkin, the pressure switch causes the filament to ignite the M-80, plus it turns on a large floodlight beamed on my porch," Mike chortled.

Mike cautions against setting the target pumpkin near where innocent children could stumble into the ambush. He tried it this past Halloween and reports the counterbullying worked wonderfully.

# Hand Grenades

These are great little framers. Let's cover the basic use plan first and then get to the decorating details. It makes a great extra for a neighborhood or community Easter egg hunt activity, or Halloween trick or treat bag, although it really will work anytime. Scatter a few of your modified hand-grenade cases around where the kiddies are likely to find one or two and bring them to mommy and daddy. Or, if you can arrange to meet some Halloweeners at your mark's home, dump one or two in the children's bags.

It won't be long until an official Police Easter Egg or Witch Hunt will begin. At the height of the panic, when the ever-present news media are there, you or your accomplice should inform some reporter (never reveal your identity) that the mark—point out his house—is a mercenary and has dozens of rifles, bombs, and grenades stored in his place.

Now, here's how to make an empty practice grenade look real. You can easily buy them with real fuse mechanisms at most surplus stores. Unscrew the top; in some grenades, though, there is already a hole in the bottom. Fill the unit with some nonexplosive (see Bombs section) which is not easily identified. Plug any holes tightly and seal with super glue. Paint over any of the blue-painted body with either flat black or olive drab paint (also available at surplus or hobby shops). Put a yellow band about half an inch wide around the neck if you wish, although not all live grenades have this band, I'm told. Screw the fuse back on, set the pop-off handle, and replace the safety pin.

Your grenade is now safely armed for some fun. But, as with the fake bogus bombs, don't get caught. This is a heavy one with the authorities despite its basically harmless prank nature.

# Ketchup

Dr. Davenport, from the town by the same name in Iowa, does not like rip-off restaurants that serve less than diet portions at porker prices. He says they are bloodsuckers, and he has found an appetizing way to deal with them.

"I carry a tampon into the restaurant. While waiting for service, I push it down into the table's ketchup bottle. Or, if I can spirit away several bottles from the service area, I fill up a few bottles. I always leave the string hanging out," says the doctor.

"I always move to a new table or another part of the establishment after doing my thing. Then I watch the ketchup customers and their reactions when they discover what I've done."

If you're worried about professional credentials to carry out this operation, don't. Dr. Davenport's hobby is amateur gynecology.

# Keyholes

My friend Bob has had a long and experienced career in the snoop 'n poop field, marred only by his own strong sense of ethics and moral honesty. He managed to share a device that must have come from the hardware division of the Nasty Toy Department: a key-in-a-sleeve device used to jam a lock, usually a door lock. The idea is to slip the bronze outer portion into any keyhole that will accept it. Turn the chromed key and remove. The bronze half is now totally "locked" in the keyhole, blocking all attempts to insert a key into the lock. Actually, the device is a secondary security lock, but it can be put to our evil uses as well.

# Keypads

According to The Stainless Steel Rat, a writer for TAP, many installations use touch-sensitive keypads as electronic locks and alarms. They are simply a numbered keyboard like a touch-sensitive phone dial, which you've no doubt seen on TV spy shows.

When nobody is around, wipe the pads free of all fingerprints, and then apply fingerprint dust on the entire surface. The next time some authorized person uses the unit, you can come forward from your observation post and discover the three- or four-digit opening code. A bit of mini-experimenting will open the unit quickly.

Or, according to the Rat, if you want to have some fun with this device, instead of beating it, just push the * and # buttons at the same time. These two buttons have a panic button or emergency function in most units, the Rat notes, and this will bring all sorts of people running.

# Landpersons

Being basically gentle folks, Americans would generally respect the rights of others. That's probably what M. Sgt. Ranger Rick, USA, thought during his days in 'Nam as a Ranger.

Despite this, M. Sgt. Rick was once sharing a basement apartment with a young lady friend. He says his upstairs neighbors belonged in a zoo. These are probably the sort from gene pools who have bruises on their knuckles from walking.

"We were had. The upstairs wife was the landlady's sister, and the landlady was shacking up with a local cop. Half the time, the cops and these broads were the ones raising hell. We had no recourse through the law, and trying gentlemanly moral persuasion didn't help either," Rick relates.

"The situation was untenable. We buried the VC in better holes than this dump. So, my friend and I had to leave at great personal inconvenience and financial loss. But, my friend and I pooled our thoughts and figured we ought to leave the place clean."

In their basement apartment stood a big water pipe that was sealed with lead rope at the joint. Rick applied hydrochloric acid just prior to their final departure from this awful abode. He says that three days later, four feet of water stood in the basement apartment. Much damage resulted, including electrical problems and structural cracking.

Obviously, this is a case of changing whine into water!

# Lawns

Here's one to help your mark harvest some wild oats. According to Sal Barclay, your local farm store sells a product known as Ortho Bugetta TM as a snail bait. Actually, this product is a hybrid oat strain that grows super fast. Some night, sprinkle it all over your mark's prize lawn. He will soon be dealing with an unusual botanical eruption.

Kilroy is obviously a lawn-lover. He suggests that some rainy night you visit your mark's lawn and spread the contents of many large boxes of corn flakes on the lawn. By morning, the mark will encounter a lawn that's full of soggy, highly unpleasant-smelling oatmeal that is very difficult to remove. If the weather stays awful, the stuff will rot the grass. If the sun comes out hot enough, it will bake it hard. Either way you have achieved serial revenge!

# Library

This trick is very simple, as outlined by Doug Hummell of Jacksontown, Pennsylvania. Go to your local library and take out a card in your mark's name. At most, all you will have to do is fill out a card with his/her name, address, etc.

The rest is simple. Take out expensive and/or rare books, and don't return them on time, or place them in your mark's home if you have access. She or he will get calls. Discovery will cause bewilderment, costly confusion and maybe court problems.

# Light Bulbs

Only someone with a wild sense of humor like my buddy Bob has could come up with this one Rube Goldberg device to break light bulbs. It's a nasty metal device with two arms tipped with sharp points. These two arms are loaded by a heavy spring. The device is attached to a light bulb, with the pincer arms held back by a cocking lever. The unit is armed by that lever, which is attached to a pull-cord. This cord is substituted for the standard pull-cord of a light fixture. When the mark goes into the darkened room and pulls the cord, *whoommmm,* all sorts of fun happens when that heavy spring that's holding back those terrible pincers is released and they explode and obliterate bulbs in less than 1/500th of a second. This stunt is very dangerous and must have originated in some strange mind at some U.S. government installation.

# Lipstick

Here's a refinement of the shoe-polish-on-the-telephone-receiver trick for marks with jealous lovers. Place a small amount of lipstick in the phone receiver. It takes such a tiny amount to do the job that the mark probably won't notice it, even if his phone is some color other than red. His or her sweetie will notice it, I guarantee that. I used this myself, and it's effective.

# Locking Gas Caps

Have a cap to spare? One of our good buddies down in Columbia, South Carolina, Andy Weiner, suggested on WIS radio that you put someone else's locking gas cap on your mark's car. It's easier for you to get a new cap for your car than it is for him to get yours off his.

# Mail

The Indiana Cave Man has a good idea with a cautionary notice.

"As a refinement to your trick of the change of address card for a mark, let's get a secondary mark with the same name. Reroute the primary mark's mail to that other person. The post office will get blamed for the mess, of course."

The Caver went on to wonder what would happen if we also filed a card sending the secondary mark's mail to the primary mark's address? Then, I wondered what would happen if you started looking for various marks with the same names in different cities?

Cave Man passes along the warning, though, that "tampering with the mails is a big crime, and postal cops are very efficient."

# Mailboxes

Millie Kemrer shares an idea that I hope doesn't get her caught in the rain, sleet, snow, or hell that falls on our U.S. mailpersons. She has a friend who displaced her mark's mailbox identity.

"A friend of mine owns a small apartment building with one really obnoxious tenant who used to get drunk and raise hell on the first and fifteenth of each month when his government checks came in. She spent hours talking to the main man without any positive results. So she simply, and illegally, removed his name from the apartment's mailbox complex. He didn't get his checks . . . or anything else. She told me he moved out."

# Mail Forwarding

My goodness, Steve has terrible handwriting, but what a wonderful mind. Here's his ample idea for helping the U.S. Postal Service deliver all their mail.

"Peel-off labels are useful. You can remove them and replace them with custom-made labels of your choice, if you follow the proper computer-looking formats. You can also remove your mark's labels if you swipe his mail. Then simply put those labels on nasty porno, religious, or other obnoxious material and mail that."

# Marks

After studying George Hayduke's books and those of his paled imitators, I figure there are five categories of mark. Knowing these differences is more than just academic; consider them to be psycho-intelligence that you can use to make your revenge either more bitter, more sweet, more fitting—or all of the above. Here are my five categories of mark.

1. ***The loser.*** This mark is dumb or innocent and rarely realizes that a zap has taken place. Your scams and stunts here call for high creativity and imagination. The potential is here, too, for long-running and continuing revenge efforts. The Loser will likely blame bad luck or his/her own personality for the misfortune(s).

2. ***Someone else, not me!*** This one is also known as the secondary mark. This secondary target is often innocent and is used only as a catalyst to wreak more revenge on the primary mark. A good example of this is to inflict an "accident" on the innocent bystander (secondary mark) in a restaurant (primary mark) when the bystander's meal, clothing, family, or property is assaulted and he/she blames the primary mark and takes action. If you're a truly cruel person, this mark is worth a lot of laughs.

3. ***Why me?*** This mark knows he or she is a victim, but the blame or evidence always points elsewhere: the dog, a stupid repairperson, a bumbling waitress, clerk, etc. Like the Loser, this type of mark rarely catches on to what's happening.

4. ***Common paranoid.*** This mark knows he or she has been the victim of some dirty trick and usually has an idea as to why. The great part is that the mark rarely knows who to blame. As the anguish intensifies, mental blocks prevent logical thought processes, creating repressive paranoid emotion. The mark's own actions at this point often cause more problems for him/her.

5. ***The game.*** This classification is based on the crude, but effective, "Godfather Syndrome," as the Indiana Cave Man terms it. The mark knows who did "it" to him or her and, usually, why it was done. Sometimes, the mark will attempt retribution. The idea is to discourage this by being awesomely awful in your choice of scams. The mark should fear trying to retaliate.

# Mealtime Guests

Davenport's Thelma wants to share a great thought that works each time. If you have guests who drop in for dinner at odd times without invitation, here's a helpful tip: Pick out the dinner plates you want to use, and smear a bit of fat on them. Just before handing the uninvited guest a plate, let your tired, old dog with the ill mouth actually lick the plates. Explain that your dishwasher is broken, and the dog is one of the family.

# Meat Loaf

Thanks to Mot Rot, I know how important meat loaf is. According to Mr. Rot, meat loaf starts out semisquishy but gets harder and harder as it sits in the leftover section of your refrigerator. Even Mr. Rot agrees that meat loaf can't be traced through ballistics, although it hurtles through the air in hardened states at great speed. Used as a blunt instrument, it can cause trauma.

# Microwave Ovens

If you have access to your mark's kitchen, remove a dozen or so raw eggs from his refrigerator and place them in the microwave oven. Set for about two minutes and quickly depart from the area.

Sometimes it pays to be nasty, not funny. According to Akron Annie, who quick-dried her ill-fated pet poodle in a microwave, you can quickly nuke one of these marvelous appliances out of order in easy fashion.

"Slide a piece of aluminum foil underneath the drip pan inside of the oven," she says. "The miracle waves do the rest. Blitzo . . . one destroyed microwave."

# Military

Ever had a cook you hated when you did KP? Here's what one "Old GI" from Florida, as he signed himself, did about it.

"This red-neck was just pure poison on KPs, pure nasty with no cause. Since it was almost always wet in the kitchen in Asia, I came up with an idea. I had seen him sprinkle a lot of foot powder in his shoes, so one day I substituted lye powder for the foot powder. In about five weeks, he was carried off that base on a stretcher and put on a plane home."

# Mobile Homes

This came in from Jimmy Carter, but he isn't the one with peanut hulls stuck to his boots by pig poop. He says if someone who lives in a mobile home, camper, or recreational vehicle gives you trouble and won't listen to reason, it's time to deflate someone's tire, although not literally.

According to Mr. Carter, using a hose clamp, attach a section of inner tube to the drain pipe on the sewage holding tank on the mark's mobile home or camper. Attach the other end, again with a hose clamp, to a device leading to the vehicle's tire or one of those emergency inflator units. When the mark flushes the potty, a great deal of pressurized sewage will literally blow up in someone's face.

# Model Aircraft

Filthy McNasty and Vera from Los Angeles have a grand air-raid number. Buy and fly a radio-controlled model airplane, or "borrow" a unit from a secondary mark. This number goes great with attacks on participants and spectators at ball games, concerts, parades, etc.

"Buzz the crowd, dive on the players, attack and ignite smoke devices or small bombs, using remote control," Vera adds.

# Neighbors

The spearhead of the Grumpy Neighbor Patrol, the redoubtable Stoney Dale, is back with another report. Stoney says you can have some innocent fun with the mark by repeatedly putting "For Sale" signs in his yard, on trees, on the porch, etc. Always advertise "Assumable 9% Mortgage" to get extra attention. If the grumpy neighbor rips down the signs, keep putting up new ones.

Here's another idea Stoney called up from his twilight zone. It works well with pseudomacho types or the Nervous Nellie person.

"In the dark of night, take a length of black fishing line and attach it to a nail or piece of the gutter support of the mark's home. Tie it low to the ground where it will be even harder to spot," Stoney advises.

"Go back and hide behind some sizable object a hundred feet or so away. Pull the line really taut. Wet your fingers and rub the line slowly, or flip the line briskly with your fingers."

Stoney says the slow rubbing produces an eerie, screeching, low-howling sound back at the house, while the line flip gives off a "boing/twang" noise.

"The person inside hears the noise and thinks it's within the walls of the house itself. If the mark comes out to look, relax the tension and let the line fall to the grass, making it invisible. When the mark retreats, repeat the devilment, as it were," Stoney adds.

A few accompanying telephone calls and other bizarre cult and mind-game stuff will contribute greatly to this screeching sound.

# Paranoia

As many readers know, folks who are into even semiserious paranoia make great marks. Put another way, markdom feeds on paranoia better than a gaggle of nursery-school kids turned loose to feed in at Mickey D's with free food coupons. But, as the Indiana Cave Man notes, a true paranoid is very dangerous because he may act first. There is some professional basis for this caution, too.

When I was in graduate school, taking a course in abnormal psychology taught by the famed professor of psychology, Dr. Kurt T. Bazz, I recall he told us that "the truly dedicated paranoid can switch from victim to aggressor very quickly if he or she strikes out first to prevent some persecution or other hostile action. . . . It is quite debatable as to whether paranoia is a cause or an effect."

I guess that means that if you really are a jerk, then someone is out to get you. If you're a bully, some people will naturally fight back. As the veteran trickster Dick Tuck relates, "Almost all deserving marks are at least slightly paranoid. And, if not, they soon will be." For example, if your mark has a paranoia about utility companies, shut down and padlock his gas or electric meter. If he or she is paranoid about trusting a spouse, twist that paranoia slowly.

One way to feed and flourish these mental hassles is to send your mark some reinforcement. I find it useful to subscribe to the U.S. Government Printing Office lists, many of which offer booklets on various personal and medical services. Catch the drift? They have publications on acne, herpes, abortions, balding, canker sores, bad breath, fat people, mental health, drug reactions, alcoholism, stress, heart attack, marital infidelity, etc. See the Sources section for the easy way to get these grand weapons.

That cheerful trickster Filthy McNasty has brought a lady friend to our merry band. Readers, say hello to Vera. However, Vera does not love a parade, and it has more to do with reality than the obnoxiousness of America's Parade Master, Ed McMahon.

"Wait until the horn and tuba section approach you," Vera relates. "Then, produce a big, juicy lemon and step out where all of the horn players can see you.

"Bite into the succulent lemon with gusto. Suck on it. Chew it wetly. Make sure they see you. This causes a universal and involuntary puckering reaction and a spinal sensation akin to nails down a blackboard. It will help rain on their parade."

Kudos to dear Vera for helping us create a sour note for the band.

Vera says this next parade-buster is really rough and should be used with discretion and thought. She suggests you toss a big, rubber snake up in front of the mark's horse. Horses react to snakes by rearing and bucking upward, tossing the rider flat on the keister.

Next on Vera's passing parade is what she calls her Smoke Screen Goody. From a chemical supply house, purchase a pint of titanium tetrachloride. Place the bottle in a paper bag. When you want to unleash mountains of smoke, place the bottle down, break it, and depart.

In a minute or so, the titanium tetrachloride will react to the air and spew tons of smoke. As Vera relates, this is the exact stuff skywriters use.

# Phone Phreaks

The guileless guru of the phone phreak is TAP, and in one of their recent numbers they included a list of ten rather irreverent suggestions for folks just like you. Here, then, is the TAP version of "The Phone Phreak's Ten Commandments."

1. Box thou not over thine home telephone wires, for those who doest must surely bring the full wrath of the Chief Special Agent down upon thy heads.
2. Speakest thou not of important matters over thine home telephone wires, for to do so is to risk thine right of freedom.
3. Use not thine own name when speaking to other Phreaks, for that every third Phreak is an FBI agent is well known.
4. Let not overly many people know that thou be a Phreak, as to do so is to use thine own self as a sacrificial lamb.
5. If thou be in school, strive to get thine self good grades, for the Authorities well know that scholars never break the law.
6. If thou workest, try to be a goodly employee, and impressest thine boss with thine enthusiasm, for important employees are often saved by their own bosses.

7. Storest thou not thine stolen goods in thine own home, for those who do are surely nonbelievers in the Bell System Security forces, and are not long for this world.
8. Attractest thou not the attention of the Authorities, as the less noticeable thou art, the better.
9. Makest sure thine friends are instant amnesiacs and will not remember that thou have called illegally, for their co-operation with the Authorities will surely lessen thine time of freedom on this Earth.
10. Supportest thou *TAP*, as it is *thine* newsletter, and without it, thy works will be far more limited.

# Photofinishing

Look through those X-rated magazines and mailers. Some of them offer wonderful ideas. For example, there is the "Adam & Eve X-Rated Photo Service" that develops those "special" pictures for you. Look for their address in my Source section. In the meantime, can you think of some ideas using these "special" pictures?

There are other outfits that sell you exposed film showing all sorts of bizarre and hardcore sexy stuff. You get it processed and it's yours. How about sending to one or more of those outfits with an order in your mark's name, including a postal money order? Switch films with your mark, and he or she will take the nasty film into some local lab. Even with mail order, it could be fun to explain to the kiddies or spouse where these graphically lustful photos came from.

Of course, you could just address the finished product to the mark's spouse or lover. I leave the rest to your imagination.

# Pious Bigots

Tim, the young scholar from the University of Texas, shares some ways to stick it to the hypocritical red-necks so common to most college towns. These cretins pray to God against students on Sunday and prey on the wallets of those same students for the rest of the week.

One particular rip-off store proprietor was also a fundamentalist preacher, according to Tim. By the way, isn't having the word "mental" in fundamental religion a contradiction in terms? Whatever, Tim said that this man's antistudent behavior became totally outrageous, and nothing logical, moral, curricular, or even secular would work to get even. So. . . .

"We got some bumper stickers printed by the brother of one of my friends who owns a print shop in another city. We placed them up high on the preacher/bigot's store and on his church, using a ladder, of course. If they (the stickers) came down, we put new ones back up again."

Tim adds that if you use a good strong glue, the stickers do not come off as easily as they otherwise might.

# Poison Ivy

Poor Bob from Panorama City! He was being sexually harassed by a female co-worker, and all sorts of nice requests to stop didn't seem to help. She was literally poisoning his own social life. He got very blunt about her leaving him alone. No luck. He decided to get even.

"I drove to the nearby hills and collected some poison ivy. I ran some stems and leaves through my food processor and collected about a cup of juice, which I placed in a plastic spray bottle. I took this to work the next morning and gave the driver's side-door handle of her car a really good shot.

"She was out of work a few days with some splotchy outbreaks in various locations. Unhappily, as soon as she got back, she was up to her old tricks again. Well, so will I, hopefully, with a less subtle message this time."

# Police Reports

Let's help our law enforcement officials make our communities better places in which to live. Find, borrow, or otherwise obtain a blank or an already-used police report form. They are fairly easy to obtain if you just think for a few moments. But, let's put one to good use. Using new Liquid Paper or some other whiting-out method, eliminate the portions already filled in if it's an old report. Type a new report, charging your mark with some horrible social crime: selling his mother-in-law into white slavery, bestiality, pimping, making bomb threats on the White House, etc. Get a very clean copy of this report and disseminate it where it will do the most good. If you can get blank report forms, you don't need any Liquid Paper.

# Porn

In view of the controversy of the TV miniseries "The Thorn Birds" in 1983, a lesson should be learned. A lot of intensely religious people really take this stuff seriously. Perhaps that belief will add to the impact of the pornography you can use to attack your mark, according to LeRoy Zimmer, one of trickery's real fans.

"I'm an amateur photographer and find it very easy to make composite photos, using the faces of very well-known religious leaders on the bodies of sexually active men engaged in very perverted activities with prostitutes, animals, and kids. I also make female religious figures unwilling participants," Zimmer says.

Following Zimmer's lead, you could create the same genre of porn by using composites featuring TV stars, top sports stars, local politicians, etc.

# Postal Service

Nobody should make his or her mail delivery person angry, but you could make one angry with a mark. Herb Bobwander says you can forge a few really nasty notes to the person who delivers the mark's mail, signing the mark's name, of course. Complain about petty, untrue things and always insult the postal employee personally and nastily. Send another letter to the postal employee's boss. Be really mean, and always sign the mark's name. It will be fun when the employee finally confronts the mark.

Johnny Zip, our mole in the Postal Service, has this tip: He lightly puts Elmer's white glue over the outside of the stamps on outgoing mail. He tells his friends to whom he's written that all they need to do to remove the cancellation marks on the stamp on their letter is to soak it in water.

Johnny can also turn this tip nasty, saying, "If you're sending mail to some mark, use lacquer, paraffin or transparent spray instead of Elmer's. This way, the cancellation marks will never adhere to the stamp at all, authorities will be suspicious, and someone will be visited by a postal inspector. Be sure to use your mark's name and another mark's return address."

If you have a mark other than the U.S. Postal Service, you might try Watergating his or her mailbox, removing personal subscription magazines, or writing insulting personal messages to the mark from "A Postal Official." Always use "official" and not "worker." Trust me, it means more fun when someone starts to investigate the complaint.

For example, if your mark gets hunting or gun magazines, you can use a Magic Marker to scrawl "KILL HUNTERS" or "SHOOT SPORTSMEN" in bold letters across the cover and on some inside pages. If your mark reads *Playboy* or a similar magazine, your message could read "YOU SEXIST PIG." If it's *Forbes,* write "WE'LL SLIT YOUR THROAT DURING THE REVOLUTION!" Maybe your mark subscribes to *High Times?* If so, he or she will probably be semi-paranoid. Try a message like "WE'RE WATCHING YOU, SUCKER" or "WE'RE POISONING YOUR DOPE." It's all very nasty, dangerous, and highly illegal. Does it surprise you, therefore, that these ideas came from Padre Patriot in Secacus, New Jersey?

If you're angry with the postal authorities for any reason, here's what Continental Paul did to get his sense of fun back. He suggests you mail a dead fish to some unknown person at some unknown address in the dead-letter office of your local post office. Eventually, reason may overrule postal regulations, and common sense might dictate that they deep-six your fishy time bomb. By then, your point will have been made.

# Potassium Permanganate

Potassium permanganate ($KMnO_4$) is a multipurpose dirty-trick chemical. Available in granular form at many drugstores, it's used as a disinfectant and for recharging water-softeners. It colors water an intense purple and later decomposes into hard-to-remove brown scum. A strong solution of this chemical will color the skin a rich chocolate brown, which lasts for days. Like fluorescein, it's great for zapping the mark's pool, aquarium, or fountain.

Potassium permanganate is also a powerful oxidizer, much like potassium nitrate, and can be used to make pyrotechnics. When the crystals are mixed with an equal volume of glycerin, it starts a fire within a few minutes. Delay time depends on temperature, mixture, purity, grain size, etc.

A friend of mine used to use permanganate/glycerin bombs in plastic pill bottles to flame trash cans at a shopping center. Another friend put one in a chemistry set in the toy department of a store that had done him wrong. Store employees thought that the chemistry set blew up all by itself, because everyone knows that chemistry sets are supposed to do that.

This same friend also sprinkled some on her friend's bath towel, and he began to dry himself off very vigorously, rubbing the little granules into his skin where they created great splotches of a hideous brown color. She said it was very funny—to her. Her friend had no sense of humor about being variegated.

# Potatoes

Stored improperly and left to rot, few things smell as awful as a potato. A retired farmer friend of mine, Mike O'Murphy, had a running feud with a coal company over their threatened ruination of his homestead water supply. Actually, his trick was more of a harassing operation at this point. Because he was being pestered by coal company lawyers, he decided that one rotten crop (the lawyers) deserved another (potatoes).

"I started to replant part of my potato harvest, one tuber at a time. I used to secrete the rotting potatoes under the lawyers' car seats when they'd drive out to the house. If I would go to their offices, I would plant a few spoiled spuds there, too. There are a few potato pranks I won't tell you about, either. Actually, it was a good use for the few spoiled spuds I had in my harvest," Mike says.

# Pricks

No, this is not scatological . . . it refers to a guy who is truly rotten to people.

Steve had a former employer who canned him for no good reason except that the boss wanted to replace him with a girlfriend he wanted on the payroll. Steve says it's a good idea to always obtain a supply of official letterhead and envelopes before you leave a company. Here's what Steve did.

"I bought an ultra sexy bra and put it into one of my old company's envelopes. I included a handwritten note to this chick about finding her bra in my car, and we were both so drunk and so horny I guess 'we' both missed it." He signed his ex-boss's name. He then addressed the letter in an incomplete fashion to a nonexistent lady at a nonexistent address. Steve mailed it.

"Naturally, it couldn't be delivered, so the postal folks returned it to the sender, the company return address with my former boss's name on the envelope. I knew his secretary, a prim, cold witch who was a snitch for his wife, would open the letter and find the bra and note. It was hilarious, or so some other employees told me later."

Buffalo's own wonderful Wayne says you should have an official-voiced caller tell the mark's lady friend that she is only one of several other women on the mark's self-confessed infection list.

"I did this, and the girl screamed and yelled to know who else was on the list," Wayne confesses. "After a while, 'the official' says that off the record he'd tell her, but she can't ever say who, how, or where, etc., to anyone. Then give her the names of a couple of close girlfriends, co-workers and/or sister, etc. If appropriate, you could even use her mother's name."

# Radio Station

Thank God there are radio stations whose DJs never answer the telephones. It makes it easier to nail naive marks. Here's how.

Find one of those stations within forty to fifty miles from the mark's home. Using press-on letters or Kroy type, create the station's call letters on stationery. Run it through a really good copy machine to create a professional forgery of the station's letterhead. On the other hand, you could borrow some real letterhead from them.

Type the mark a letter indicating that he or she has won some fabulous prize from a lottery drawing. The ticket was bought by ________________ (use the name of some friend who is on vacation or otherwise unavailable). The letter must indicate that the prize is substantial—$1,000 in cash, a TV, VCR, stereo, whatever. Also be sure to note that the prize must be *personally* claimed within two days.

Here's why you selected a station whose DJs never answer the phone: Instruct the mark to call between the hours of 7 P.M. and 11 P.M. because those are the only hours the "promotion" lines are open.

Getting no answer, the mark will either (1) worry about it, (2) drive the forty or fifty miles to personally collect, or (3) call during the day and make a fool of himself or herself. You could also claim that personal claim must be made within twenty-four hours, and there is no need to confirm.

# Religion

Are you the victim of door-to-door Bible sellers? Our own Trab from Houston has a fabulous bit of theater that is a devastating example of overcope.

"Answer the door wearing a deep-black mask with red streaks. Open the door slowly, and peer out at the person around the door. Listen to the pitch, which will probably be nervous at best. Interrupt and say, 'Yes, my dear, I have a contribution, a very fresh one.' At that point, introduce what is in your other hand, hidden behind the door—a freshly obtained animal heart, beef tongue, or something equally gross from the meat market which you had all set up," advises Trab.

"As an alternative, you can answer the door in your underwear and have blood and animal slick all over your chest, face, and belly (as if you were eating some fresh sacrifice). Invite the mark to join you," chortles Trab.

According to the wonderful Sister Carla of the Order of St. Hedon, there are some special ways to produce counterproductive activities at an establishment religious service. I have known Sister Carla for some time, and she is a wonderful, sweet person with some delightful ideas, which she radiates from her Southern California retreat. Her suggestions for activity follow:

1. You and a friend can walk into a cathedral as a couple wearing clerical robes. Remove them, and do a streak during the ceremony.
2. Enter the church with a joint in your hand and tell the preacher that it's not sinful to smoke grass because the Bible says, "Let there be grass!"
3. Plant marijuana in the churchyard.
4. Pie the preacher while he is giving his boring sermon.
5. Open a large, noisy bag of potato chips or Nachos and make a lot of noise while eating them during the ceremony.
6. Pull a false fire alarm during a church service, thereby disrupting the service.
7. Buy an ad in the local smut paper advertising the church's phone number as being that of an out-call massage parlor.
8. Enter a synagogue with a pig on a leash.
9. Enter a church disguised as the devil.
10. Hand the preacher a hypodermic needle and a bag of white powder, telling him that "religion is the opiate of the masses."

# Remail Service

You don't have to pay a fortune to remail letters from other cities. Having a mail-drop service is a great tool, but you don't need it for remailing. The cost of first-class postage, two envelopes and a short note will do the job. Write what you want to whomever you want. Address the envelope as you wish and seal the letter. Put the postage on it and a straight-looking return address. Write a brief note to the Postmaster in the city or town you've selected to remail this letter. Ask him to please *forward* this for you (don't ask for remail; ask for it to be *forwarded*). Slip the note and letter into a second envelope addressed to the Postmaster in that city. Use the same return address. Put postage on that outside envelope, mail it, and await the results. There is nothing illegal or immoral in this.

# Restaurants

Bob Grain always carries a collection of newly dead waterbugs and cockroaches with him for inclusion in his plans to get back at eateries which gastrate him. Bob says he tapes the little bodies to the menu or several bugs to several menus in his least favorite restaurants. At the very worst, you'll get some guy who will strip off the tape and eat the bug, figuring it was some free hors d'oeuvre sample.

# Résumés

The following trick works well in a large company with a central copy or office services room. If you can get a copy of your mark's résumé (if not, make one up), leave a copy around the copy machine for the office gossips to find. If that's not enough, read on.

You can have a printer friend produce letterheads using some name and address to represent a professional employment agency. Type a cover letter on this letterhead to accompany a copy of your mark's résumé, both of which will be sent to his or her present boss. The cover letter should state that the mark is very unhappy working with unprofessional, cheap dolts and wants to escape his current enslavement. The mark's boss will get a big bang out of reading this letter, and so might the mark . . . later.

# Ritual Madness

Many ethnic food markets cater to customers who like to eat goat and sheep heads, bull testicles, beef tongue, Bulgarian toe jam plus other exotic delights. Much of this stuff looks like central casting's idea of horror film gore. I thought I might catch your interest here, as these items are truly useful.

Heidi Marie says these culinary catastrophes make wonderful combinations with a devilish imagination to drive a mark wild with fear.

"Imagine how an occult sacrifice would look on the mark's doorstep—not only to the mark, but to the neighbors as well. You can use any of the animal heads, bushels of entrails, and blood, plus you should always include a doll or some other symbol for a baby in this ritual," Heidi advises.

# Roadkill

Although George Hayduke institutionalized the concept of roadkill, some of his biker buddies went further when they created a cooked version called Furry Curry. I'm a genteel person, and I was moved.

According to Henry Zeybel, writing in *Easyriders,* Furry Curry is made from the "tiny roadside creatures which have paid the ultimate price of the machine age." He adds, "Any sharp-eyed rider can find roadside delicacies to supplement his dinner table."

Here's one of his excellent recipes that helps us use our deceased little forest friends to recycled advantage.

1. Scrape up whatever it was, and strip off any of the outer cover that's left.
2. Soak what remains in salt water for a couple days.
3. Whatever isn't already hamburger should be cut into half-inch cubes and sauteed until medium. What is semihamburger should be smashed with a hammer, molded into patties, and stored.
4. For the rest, melt butter and mix in onions, garlic cloves, lemon juice, curry powder, and brown sugar.

5. Stir until you have one big lumpy mass. At this point, dump in a pint of sour cream and stir until the sauce looks like bile.

If the sauce is not thick enough, add some gun grease and shortening. I'm told this will feed ten squeamish straights or one righteous biker.

# Salespeople

Want to get rid of pushy salespeople who sell with all the couth and subtlety of a high-pressure, crowd-control hose? Ron from Florida has the answer.

"I was seriously interested in a resort condo, but I really resented the unfair sales-pressure tactics, especially on older people who got a bit confused and fearful. I decided to get even.

"I acted like the perfect customer. I really took up the salesman's time, and this pushy creep had it all down. I asked questions for hours and then we got to the fine print and the terms. I was totally agreeable and talked about my banker, lawyer, etc.

"The pushy man went to his superior because I was buying three units, and they worked out the entire deal. We're talking several hours of their expensive time. Me? I was on vacation, and this was fun.

"At the last minute, after they'd signed and handed me the pen, I looked at them, smiled and said, 'Ah, heck, I was just kidding,' put down the pen, turned and walked away. I never looked back but I could feel the daggers of frustration and hate at my back."

# Shampoo

Some popular shampoo products resemble a thick, white milky solution. There are many interesting additives that will blend with and hold in these shampoos without being easily detected (Elmer's glue, Nair, and Resin).

# Shaving Cream

Durango Bob used to belong to a fraternity, I bet. Or at least, he was in a swinging dormitory. Here's his idea of big fun. Take a manila envelope and fill it with shaving cream. Slit open one end, and shove it under the mark's door. Knock on the door and get down low so you can see the mark's shoes approaching. Quickly line up the envelope, stand up, and stomp down on your end of the cream-filled bag, squirting all the glop on the mark's shoes. Run like hell. You could also substitute other squishy things for the shaving cream.

# Sinks

This scam is known as the Fishbein Effect, as it is named for Dr. Chunder H. Fishbein, a noted rhetorician at the Wanker Institute of Anti-Semantic Behavior in Fulco-on-the-Hudson, New York.

"Use black electrical tape to close down the handle on the spray hose at your mark's kitchen sink. Make sure the hose nozzle is pointing out toward the middle of the sink, and then ask your mark for a glass of water. If that is not appropriate, just wait for the action to take place."

Interestingly, according to his notes, this same idea came during a radio talk show from a young lady named Jenny in Orlando, Florida.

# Slime

Not only is this a wonderful name to call people, it is a commercial product available in toy and variety stories. It's sort of a runny variation of Silly Putty, as one wag put it. The potential of this stuff is awesome. It can be used to gross out and sabotage marks, and to play messy mind games.

For example, you can put some Slime in the coin return of a pay telephone or in earphones. It is also an unwelcome addition to stereo headphones. It makes a nice complement to a salad bar. When combined with butyric acid, it goes on meat as a sauce. Perhaps a drool of it could come off your nose, ear, mouth, or some other orifice, which you could direct at your mark, especially if same has a queasy stomach. The uses of Slime are bountiful, indeed, and we should all thank its maker by buying and spreading Slime around.

# Slippery Stuff

Yes, you, the ordinary citizen, can order "Instant Banana Peel" from police supply houses. It's a chemical which is dusted on the road and wetted with water. It then becomes slippery as the dickens, so much so that nobody can walk on it. Police use it for skid pans and riot control. You can use it for parades, street games, classes, dances, etc.

# Smoke

"Smokey the Bare" says that where there's smoke, there might just be Liquid Smoke, the stuff you use when you cook hamburgers, steaks, etc., and want that outdoor, hickory-smoke flavor.

"Just think how your mark's car would smell if you doused a good shot of Wright's (Liquid Smoke) all over the inside. How would that seem to a prospective buyer if the mark were a car dealer? It could easily work in an office, home, or apartment, too," Smokey informs us. "The best part is that this liquid contribution to your trickster's revenge kit is universally available in any supermarket, and it is innocent looking, yet so easy to use."

# Snot

This reminds me of those ball players or old farmers who always blew their noses out in the field. According to Mr. Charlie, the method is to stuff one nostril shut with an index finger and then clear the other nostril with a mighty blow of air. Switch to the other nostril and then tidy up with your shirt sleeve.

A bartenderess I know, Bonnie Woodland, uses this old tactic to deal with obnoxious customers she cannot otherwise insult. "I uncap the jerk's beer, and while bent over the cooler unobserved I clear my nose into his open beer. I then pour it for him, and he never notices my additives because of the foam."

# SOBs in General

Write an endorsement letter, make a phone call, or otherwise publicly support every nut, idiot, dictator, crook, jerk, killer, psychopath, etc., that you can think of—all in your mark's name. It's much better if you can use his/her official letterhead, or you can make up official-looking stationery. This is a great idea, thanks to wonderful M. K. of Long Beach. May I add some suggestions? Do this in newspapers, and write to government officials and others in the public eye. Be outspoken, obnoxious, and demanding—all in your mark's name, naturally.

You might wish to start a file on your mark with some government agency. Start writing threatening letters and/or writing "good citizen" letters to various state and federal government agencies for and about your mark. The more rotten your imagination, the better the letter, I bet.

# Sources

There are many willing or innocent businesses or sources which can be a great help to you. Here are just a few for you to contact:

Adam & Eve X-Rated Photo Finishing. Carborro, NC 27510.

AMC Sales. P.O. Box 928, Downey, CA 90241.
They sell long-playing recorders, mikes, and bugging and debugging stuff.

Bowyer, J. Barton, *Cheating*. (New York: St. Martin's Press, 1983).
This is a funny book, and it's a bit of an in-house deception itself. The "author" is actually two people, both respected political/military/intelligence analysts. The book is a monument to great hoaxers and cheaters—an overview of scamdom. It's a very worthwhile book for someone who wants to get into the philosophy of this stuff.

Chemtek. P.O. Box 573, Hawkesbury, Ontario, Canada.
They feature very-hard-to-obtain chemicals, and you'll see why when you deal with them.

Delta, Ltd. P.O. Box 777, Mt. Ida, AR 71957.
Publisher of survival and weapons materials and books. Also bumper and door stickers with a real social message, part of our lives, of course. But, Delta, Ltd., has a difference. They advertise "Put a warning on your door that even *criminals* can't ignore."

Howelab Company. P.O. Box 73, Folly Beach, SC 29439.
They sell smoke bombs, skunk and other animal scent, urine, etc. It's good stuff, too.

Law Enforcement Associates, Inc. P.O. Box 128, Bellview, NJ 17109.
Their service is high-tech security equipment . . . very professional.

Northern Hydraulics. P.O. Box 1219, Burnsville, MI 55337.
These people sell all sorts of grand industrial and agricultural products and equipment. Their extensive catalog displays a wonderous treasure of trickery hardware.

Reliance Group. P.O. Box 4582, Stockton, CA 95204.
They do remailing and custom-made IDs. They are very trustworthy and professional.

Survival Books & Supply. 11106 Manglia Blvd., North Hollywood, CA 91601.
They have the library and equipment to match their name.

TAP. Room 603, 147 W. 42nd St., New York, NY 10036.

As always, these folks have all the latest word on phreaking and other forms of electronic trashing of the establishment.

Tech-Group. P.O. Box 3125, Pasadena, CA 91103.

Mail forwarding, remailing, payments, collections, dead service, safe houses, equipment and vehicle rental, etc.

U.S. General Supply Corp. 100 Commercial Street, Plainview, NY 11803.

Get your supply of stump rot from these folks.

U.S. Government Printing Office. Washington, D.C. 20401.

This wonderful outfit contains innumerable weapons in your antimark warfare. To see what and how, write and get on their catalog lists.

Walter Drake & Sons. Drake Building, Colo. Springs, CO 80940.

They custom-print bumper stickers, letterhead, and return-address stickers. This one could be a gold mine. The cost is $4 for the first sticker and 75¢ for each additional one.

# Speakers

Speakers, and often amplifiers as well, can be destroyed by connecting their terminals to the 117-volt power line. The Indiana Cave Man adds that if you can't get at the wiring of the mark's loud stereo or PA/background music system, use a razor blade or sharp knife to sever the wire between the voice coil in the middle of the speaker and the spots on the back of the cone where heavier wires are attached.

Also, speakers and some types of microphones can be ruined by iron filings placed in the magnet gap. In some models, you must pierce the flexible barrier covering the gap to introduce the filings. Cut-up fibers of fine steel wool work best and are also effective for shorting out amplifiers, TV sets, computers, and other electronic equipment. Put the fibers in a flexible plastic tube, insert one end into the appliance, and blow.

# Spouses

One of my good friends in Pennsylvania caught a guy messing around with his girl. Know what he did to get even? He let the guy marry her!

# Stickers

If you want to slow customer traffic to a particular store for some justified reason, have your printer prepare some fairly large stickers for you. The backing should be as permanent-stick as possible. Keep placing your sticker near the stickers at store entrances which explain shoplifting policies, business hours, etc. Your sticker will say "WARNING. ANYONE WEARING A PACEMAKER IS PROHIBITED FROM USING THIS ELECTRONIC ENTRANCE."

WARNING
TRESPASSERS
WILL BE SHOT
SURVIVORS
WILL BE SHOT AGAIN

NEVER MIND
THE DOG.
BEWARE OF
OWNER!

IS THERE LIFE
AFTER DEATH?
TRESPASS HERE
AND FIND OUT

NOTICE
ANYONE FOUND HERE
AT NIGHT
WILL BE FOUND HERE
IN THE MORNING

# "Stopper"

This wonderful invention comes to us courtesy of The Tennessean, who suggests many marvelous uses for it. Essentially, "The Stopper" is a two- or three-inch square of wall panel through which five to eight large roofing nails are pushed. The Stopper is then laid on a road or path, sharp end up, and covered with loose gravel, dirt, or leaves. Our patron says they make wonderful welcoming mats for trail bikers, motorized hunters, and others who trespass on your property.

Use several at a time, and spread them out. As The Tennessean says, "Most cars carry one spare, but that doesn't help three flats. Bikers rarely have a spare tire."

# Students

If you've ever starred in the role of college student, you know the act of hiring someone to write a term paper for you. You might even know someone you hate who always writes wonderful papers, even when hung over, or you hate the class snob for being so proper and getting As without making any effort, so here's how to get back.

One suggestion is to wait until the mark has placed his or her paper on the pile on the teacher's desk, when you can then go to the stack of papers and remove the mark's original paper. Use common sense on your approach to this.

Then, we have the scam. Replace the mark's own paper with a specially written new one. This new one contains all the elements guaranteed to garner an "F" grade. You should also be sure to include several personal references to the professor or some unjustified ethnic and racial charges, too.

# Stump Rot

You see this miracle product advertised everywhere from Sunday newspapers to backyard gardener magazines. Simply pour it onto the stump or into holes you've drilled into the stump, and the stump just sort of shrivels away. A product with that potential is just too good to pass up in a book of this sort.

In the event you can't find an advertisement of your own, I am looking at just such a catalog ad this very moment (see Sources section).

# Success Stories

There's a disciple of chicanery living in Pittsburgh, who was written up in the local newspaper. According to the newspaper, Jude Pohl is a "true patron of lost consumer causes. He does not rant and rave. He does not slink off. He is the soul of quiet persistence . . . Invariably, he gets justice."

That's our kind of person!

The feature article told how Pohl took on supermarkets, film companies, loan companies, and other giant corporations that usually stomp all over us little folks.

Do we have a fan in San Jose also? Early in 1983, wonderfully uptight San Jose experienced a scam that not only destroyed some mark's home, but also cheated seventy-five men out of a payday. It seems someone called the California State Employment Development Department, the out-of-work-helpers, in January to "hire" seventy-five men to tear down a vacant house in East San Jose. The work had to be fast.

It was.

It was also cheap. And, the man who owned the house wasn't the man who made the call. The owner showed up in shock when his place was down to its foundation.

The call was a hoax. The owner was out one house, and those seventy-five workers were out some thirty dollars. Meantime, someone else was having a real laugh.

In Gibraltar, Michigan, hundreds of pictures depicting a Brownstown Township school secretary in sexual acts were mailed to schools and businesses and scattered along a street, police told Associated Press.

Children reported finding the pictures on their way to a suburban Detroit elementary school, according to the AP report. The pictures were inscribed with the woman's name and address.

"It is likely that a picture of the woman's face had been superimposed on the photos," said local police Sgt. Dan Grant.

During WWII, the OSS found that sugar in the gas tank is not a reliable way to sabotage motor vehicles. The myth is universally believed, however, which is good mind-bender news. Instead, save your empty sugar sacks. Drop one on the ground near the mark's vehicle and sprinkle a handful of sugar on the ground under the gas-tank filler. The mark will be afraid to start the engine until the fuel system is purged. It's cheaper and faster than actually sweetening the fuel, and it causes almost as much grief.

It must. According to the Indiana Cave Man, he once incapacitated an entire herd of earthmovers belonging to the U.S. Army Corps of Engineers, which was working at a land-raping site.

"All I used was half a dozen, empty five-pound sugar sacks with a bit of residue scattered around the machines and the ground under the fuel tanks," he notes.

# Suitmen

Suitmen are the three-piece corporate types who are the lounge lizards who stalk and prey during Happy Hour. Our friend Kilroy has a rather involved and potentially destructive sting for these flesh-feasting marks.

Check in your local library for the Thomas Register, and find the name of two of the major competitors of your mark's company. Next, get letterhead and envelopes from the mark's company, or create them by using some of the more sophisticated versions of PressType. Let's say he works for the Worthen Widget Company of Bumjump, Georgia. The two competitors are Mighty Manufacturing Inc., of Chicago, and Widget Master of Broomfield, Colorado. Address a letter to Widget Master, using the Chicago address of the second competitor. Also, find and use the name of an actual executive at Widget Master to whom you should address your letter.

Obviously, the post office in Chicago will not be able to locate any such company as Widget Master, and they will return the letter to the sender. It will no doubt be opened by some company secretary, unless you specifically direct the return address to a certain office, which may prove advantageous.

Why is all of this nasty? When the person at Worthen Widgets opens the returned letter, to see where to direct it, here is what it will say:

WORTHEN WIDGET
COMPANY LOGO
ADDRESS

Mr. John E. Presser
Widget Master Company
Chicago, Illinois

Dear John,

Please forward the $15,000 payment we agreed upon last month for the manufacturing data and new product specs I furnished you. Come on, man, we had a deal, remember?

Sincerely,

I. M. Mark

Naturally, an incendiary letter like this will make the rounds of corporate powerdom very quickly, especially if Mr. Mark is an unpopular chap. Also, the mix-up of two companies and towns will cause some suspicion that Mr. Mark was dealing double. All in all, he's on his way down the corporate crapper. This stunt has about a seventy-percent kill(roy) ratio.

# Super Glue

A sharing reader from Huntsville, Alabama, shared a takeoff (no pun) on the old super-glue/male member stunt. A lady caught her husband cheating again after repeated warnings. After a few nights of nonfighting, she let him sleep peacefully. After gently arousing him sexually in his sleep, she quietly and carefully coated his fingers with super glue, handed him his penis, and then intertwined his fingers around it. According to our Huntsville agent, the chap had to go into surgery for corrective action.

# Super Glue Bombs

Here's a truly funny idea from Kilroy. We're all aware of what the mail-order trade calls bubble packing. You can make messy bombs with that stuff, something that could stick with your mark for days.

The idea is to cut out one individual bubble from the sheet and puncture a hole, one sixteenth of an inch, in the bubble. Inject Eastman 910 into that hole and fill the bubble. The hole will seal itself, and you have a tiny glue bomb. Place these little nasties in people's shoes, clothes, bedding, pants pockets, seats, etc.

If you tire of sticking it to your mark, you could use other additives to fill the little bombs.

# Supermarket

California's Mot Rot puts some practical ideas to work. Do they work? According to Mot, one very deserving rip-off supermarket in a "nearby" town got sued for selling dead cats (packaged in store wrapping), in their meat section.

"I wonder who the stockperson was who put the fataled felines in there?" Mot says with a wild laugh.

# Swimming Pools

Our old friend Stoney Dale had a bad time at a very snotty country club when the elite made sport of his humble origins. Undaunted, he came back that night with a couple of chocolate candy bars and tossed them into the sacred swimming pool—after unwrapping them.

"The pool was drained the next day because officials were certain the pool had been used as an unauthorized commode," Stoney reports.

I bet if you laid some toilet paper around the pool area, as well as in the pool, it would add to the illusion.

# Talk Mongers

An Iowa lady who worked two shifts during the Depression of 1982-83, told me she had a friend who used to call her and chat at 7 A.M.

"She had to go to work at 8:30, so she called me at 7:30 to talk. I worked two shifts to keep my kids fed, clothed, and housed, and I had no time for this silly broad. I tried to explain this to her, but it never sunk in.

"My idea was simple. My sister was in college in California and worked the day shift, so I asked her to call my 'gabby friend' at 4 or 5 in the morning and repay the favor. It worked. I got an apology from her, and we became better friends."

# Tape Recordings

If you have a tape recording of your mark's voice that contains enough words and you have a lot of editing time on your hands, you can splice together a delightfully rotten, obscene call featuring your mark. Dial a family member or a second mark. When the target answers, push the Play button on your machine and let Mark I say it all to Mark II. This friendly idea comes to you courtesy of Darrell W. Woffard.

You can also add your own lyrics to someone else's music. Jimi the Z says to borrow a "Vocal Zapper," a forty-dollar gadget which filters out the vocals on recordings, leaving all the instrumentals untouched. Next, use your own lyrics, using your imagination and mark's susceptibility in regard to content (crude, political, outlandish, gross, sexual, etc.). Zap the original vocals on a standard recorded tune, and dub your own, new vocals, or get someone who can sing to do it for you. You can then disseminate your new vocals for this standard tune over PA systems, Muzak, radio, etc.

# Tenants

I believe in landlords. Well, some landlords, anyway, as I have been one myself. Anyway, this nice man, Jason, from St. Simons Island in Georgia, wrote to explain how he handled the other side of the landlord/tenant dispute.

"As a landlord, you get stuck with a lot of unsavory and deadbeat tenants. It seems that legal rights go against us landlords. But, if you want someone out, I found a perfectly legal way to do it. I've done it, and it works.

"Most laws say you cannot lock a tenant out. There are no laws about unlocking the tenant, though. I send my unsavory tenant, what you call a mark, a registered letter saying that new locks are to be installed for security purposes. I always make sure to appear personally and give the tenant the new keys before the operation takes place.

"I am a rotten carpenter, and you just can't get good help, so I personally remove the door to that tenant's apartment and take it away for lock-changing. I am such a bad worker that I might not get that door back for five or six days. Sometimes, really bad people could come into the tenant's apartment and steal things. Often these people are the tenant's friends. Nice folks. Great scheme. It works," Jason notes.

# Things that Smell Bad

If your mark happens to be a business or organization with public bathrooms, here's something that will give you a few laughs. Locate the paper-towel machine, and note the names of the manufacturer and the model number. Later, write to them on some official letterhead and ask for a duplicate key. Say your janitor lost yours. Send them a couple dollars cash for it.

When you get the key, enter the mark's rest room, unlock the towel machine and remove it from the wall via the screws located inside. Chip a hole in the wall behind the unit. Insert a dead fish or piece of chicken in that hole, and replace the dispenser. Clean up all the mess on the floor and leave.

According to Kilroy, if you don't want to leave so permanent a smell, you can simply unlock the unit and place the offending odor-maker in there with the towels. In that case, happy, happy face-wiping, secondary marks!

# Time Bombs

Doug Draut passes along the plans for a nifty time bomb that odorizes your mark's home, car, apartment, office, etc. Doug says to use empty cold capsules and fill them with baking soda. Put some vinegar in a plastic bag. Drop the capsules in, and fill the bag with air. Seal it. Break open the capsules inside the bag and quickly drop it in the mark's property. The gas causes the bag to rupture, causing the smelly vinegar to leak everywhere.

# Toasters

Once more, my friend Kilroy is the toast of the tome. He says that such a simple device as a kitchen toaster lends itself well to the deviant imagination.

"Look down inside your toaster," Kilroy says. "Notice the heating elements that turn bright red when the toaster is turned on. These elements can easily become a detonator for the fuses of firecrackers or smoke bombs. Or, you can hang rubber bands on these elements to cook up an especially obnoxious odor."

# Toilets

I don't know why so many people, especially little boys of all ages, find toilets so funny. But, bathroom humor is very big. C. W. from Hastings, Nebraska, has a trick we could label the "Heinz squirts." But, let's let C. W. tell the story.

"Take one of those little plastic ketchup or mustard containers, or one of each, that you get in fast food places. Lift the seat off the mark's toilet. Slice the top of each container and set it gently on the edge of the porcelain toilet below the seat. Orient it so the packages line up with the seat knobs. Gently—very gently—put the seat down.

"When the mark sits down, *splooey, spooley, spoooooly* . . . the packages will squirt their contents all over the mark's behind, legs, pants, jeans, or whatever. This trick works great with females, of course."

The mark in this case might just be a bar, restaurant, hotel, gas station, or public place. Or it could be a private residence.

According to Ann Nonymous and her friend, a toilet can be a great mind-bender, too. They advise you to call your mark on the telephone, pour a pitcher of water into the handy commode, holding the telephone so the mark will hear this. Flush the facility loudly so the mark will hear the flushing. Laugh softly into the phone, or tell the mark that's what will happen to him, etc. Now hang up. You may repeat this at random intervals if you feel the mark has not been flushed enough. It makes many paranoid marks very nervous.

Kilroy had this idea for a mark's porcelain throne. Locate the main water shut-off valve outside the mark's home (if the shutoff is inside, you'll have to sneak into the house). Torque it to the full open position with a wrench, and then run a bead of super glue around the shaft of the valve so it can't turn at all.

You need to get into the mark's home in order to carry out the next step in the commodious chicanery. Once there, do the exact same thing to the valve directly connected to the thunder jug itself. Remove the cover on the toilet tank and unscrew the float on the float valve. Be sure to leave the tank float in position, though. Touch a few beads of super glue around the edge of the tank—don't use a full bead as it might form a waterproof seal. Replace the cover.

Flushed with success, you can now await your mark's first operation of the tampered toilet. Within minutes, he or she will be doing a wild Moses, trying to part the overflowing effluvial sea.

# Toll Roads

A man named Ron from Florida advises paying toll-road fees by check if your mark is the highway system, the state, the toll road, or the collector. It's all quite legal and a hell of a hassle, especially if it's for a small amount. It involves a lot of red tape, I.D. checking, and time wasted while other motorists get impatient. But it is legal, and you can explain that you have no cash with you. (PS: It's good to stash away fifty dollars in the glove compartment in the event the law comes down on you for retribution further on down the road.)

# Travel Plans

If you've ever played airport roulette, you know how easy it is to cancel or alter your own flight plans. Did you ever consider doing it to or for someone else? You might sometimes need a lot of information for this, like names, dates, destinations, card numbers, etc., but if you do it during busy times, the airline people rarely check too much. Be sure to gather as much information on the mark as possible.

# Twist-off Bottle Lids

You can have a lot of fun with people who have to live with twist-off caps. Simply turn the bottle upside down, thinly bead some super glue or Eastman 910 around the rim, let it dry, and turn it upright.

The resultant damage is called Belted Biceps Biopsy.

# Video Games

Fred Steinbeck passes along some freak news about efforts to infiltrate video games.

This trick isn't exactly new, but in some video games a small flaw in the coin totalizer allows free games. Take a small but weighty object such as a "D" size battery or pocket knife, and give the machine a sharp rap between the coin-deposit and coin-return slots. If you have done it correctly, you will get one free credit. Do it more, and get more. There's no law of diminishing returns here! However, some machines have been fitted with a "tilt" switch, so, ya win some, ya lose some.

Agent NDS tells of a free-game trick on the Junior Donkey Kong machine. Take a flattened straw and insert it about three inches along the right-hand crack between the cash box and the machine, about two to three inches down from the top crack between the cash box and the machine, and wiggle the straw up and down. You will rack up some credits.

# Welding Compound

This is basically a cold weld product that lets you make all sorts of "repairs" around the home and office. It "repairs, fills and bonds iron, brass, pewter, aluminum, steel, copper, and bronze." I'm not at all mechanical, but I can think of all sorts of things your mark might need to have "repaired." This product is available from U.S. General Supply Corp. (See Sources section.)

# Windows

Deadeye Jordan passes along a true CIA-style act that enables you to take out a glass window without leaving evidence of any projectile. He advises you to use a Whamo wrist rocket slingshot and a small, clear-glass marble as a projectile. Both the target window and the projectile marble will shatter, leaving no evidence. Sonic boom, UFOs or the Trilateral Commission will get the blame.

# Windshield Wipers

Obtain a handful of aluminum oxide micro grit from a chemistry supply source. On a drizzly, but not real rainy, day, pour a bead of this grit on the wiper blades of your mark's car. When he or she turns on the wipers, the grit will severely scratch the windshield.

# Word for the Day

One of the worst jokes I ever heard came from the infamous Gerald Anderson, clown prince of Woodland and conductor of the Mt. Lebanon Wind Symphony, who tells you authoritatively that the word for the day is "legs." Then, with a shy smile, he says, "Help spread the word."

# Yellow Pages

There are some businesses that thrive on letting people's fingers do the walking. Some businesses depend on the Yellow Pages. If your mark has such a business, you might just help him or her along to court. Here's dependable old Kilroy's advice.

"For this you need access to your mark's business telephone or at least the outside terminals. The idea is to make last-minute changes in Yellow Pages advertising. You call in the changes or the cancellation at the *very last* minute. You will probably be asked to furnish the mark's account number, too, so be prepared for that.

"In my experience with this scam, they usually call the mark's number right back to verify. Here's where you and/or an associate have to have command of that telephone or number so that you can be the one to verify the changes.

"It works. I had to use this on a professional person a few years ago as payback for some very costly things that happened to me thanks to his incompetency and absolute refusal to make good. My revenge worked perfectly," Kilroy says.

# Zulu

That's the last letter in the phonetic alphabet and the last word in this collection, but not *my* last word. Please send me your contributions of nasty tricks for my next book.